*To Kathy Callaghan and Helen Chambers—
wise keepers-of-ritual
and person-affirmers extraordinaire.*

By virtue of the Creation and,
still more, of the Incarnation,
nothing here below is *profane*
for those who know how to see.

—Pierre Teilhard de Chardin
The Divine Milieu

CONTENTS

Introduction *1*

Chart of Incarnation Season Dates *4*

Advent *7*

First Sunday of Advent

A Time of Beginnings 8
A Time of Counting Down 10
A Time of Isaiah 11
A Time of Stories 13
A Time of Maranatha! 15
A Time of Planning Christmas Celebrations 16
A Time of Kind Words 19

Second Sunday of Advent

A Time of Preparation 21
A Time of Music 22
A Time of Sharing 24
A Time of Shopping 25
A Time of Mary and Martha 27
A Time of Darkness and Light 28
A Time of Gifting 30

Feast of the Immaculate Conception (December 8)

A Time of the Magnificat 32

Hanukkah

A Time of Kinship 34

Third Sunday of Advent

A Time of Joy 36
A Time of Gifts 37
A Time of Graciousness 39
A Time of Blessing 41
A Time of Silence 42
A Time of Panic 44
A Time of Matthew 46

Fourth Sunday of Advent

A Time of Children 48
A Time of Expectation 49
A Time of Faith 51
A Time of the Infancy Narratives 52
A Time of Luke 54
A Time for the 'O Antiphons' 56
A Time of 'Yes!' 57

Christmas *61*

Christmas Day (December 25)

Celebrating Love 62

Feast of St. Stephen (December 26)

Celebrating the Gospel's Challenge 64

Feast of St. John (December 27)

Celebrating the Word 66

The Holy Innocents (December 28)

Celebrating the Life-Death Journey 68

The Days of Christmas

Celebrating Church 70
Celebrating Traditions 71

Celebrating Surprises 73
Celebrating Symbols 74
Celebrating Thanksgiving 76
Celebrating Visits 77
Celebrating the Magi 79

Feast of The Holy Family

Celebrating Family 81

New Year's Eve (December 31)

Celebrating Memory 83

New Year's Day (January 1)

Celebrating Mary 85

Epiphany 87

Epiphany

Celebrating God-Made-Manifest 88
A Time of Preaching 89
A Time of Reality 90
A Time of Storytelling 92
A Time of Time 94
A Time of Visions 95
A Time of Secrets Revealed 97

Feast of the Baptism of the Lord

Ordinary Time: A Time of Growth and Proclamation 99

Incarnation Season Projects and Gifts 103

Projects for Families and Individuals

For the Entire Incarnation Season 104
For Advent 107
For the Days of Christmas 108
For Epiphany 110

Projects for Groups and Organizations

Gift Suggestions

For Everyone and Anyone   112
*For the Hard to Please or the Person Who 'Has
   Everything'   113*
For the Homebound or the Financially Distressed   114
For Yourself   114
For Special People   114

Prayers for the Incarnation Season   *117*

Biblical Prayers

Canticle of Mary (Luke 1:46-55)   118
Canticle of Zechariah (Luke 1:68-79)   119
Canticle of Isaiah (Isaiah 9:1-6)   120
Canticle of the Angels (Luke 2:14)   121
Canticle of Simeon (Luke 2:29-32)   121

Traditional Prayers

The Hail Mary   121
The Angelus   122
The Joyful Mysteries of the Rosary   123

Seasonal Prayers

The Advent Wreath   123
Advent Wreath Prayers   124
Blessing of the Christmas Tree   129
A Thanksgiving Service   130
Christmas Gifts   131
'O Antiphons'   132
Blessing of a Home   133

INTRODUCTION

C hristmas—the twenty-fifth day of December— comes each year. It comes whether we observe it or ignore it. It comes whether our response is "Alleluia!" or "Bah, humbug!"

But *Christ's coming* is another matter. Christ's coming into our lives demands our involvement. We must be open to it, recognize it, respond to it. And it is this coming of Christ that is the focus of what I call the Incarnation Season. Our celebration of the Incarnation not only recognizes the birth of the historical Christ; it is also our celebration of the risen, cosmic Christ in our lives today and our anticipation of the Second Coming of Christ. We have much to celebrate!

Fortunately, a holy celebration of the Incarnation does not require that we separate ourselves from the world around us, for the Incarnation itself is a call for us to recognize the sacredness of this world into which Christ was born. It is a time to recognize the sacramentality of everyday life.

That's why being busy during the holidays is not necessarily contrary to the spirit of the season. The very complexity of modern life helps us realize that the busier we are, the more we need prayer and meditation to sustain us in our busyness and to remind us of the reasons that validate that busyness. The more items on our to-do list, the greater our need of God's help in ordering those items with wisdom.

The reflections, projects and prayers presented

here are gift-wrapped in the hope that they may help increase for you both the enjoyment and blessedness of this most wonderful season.

HOW TO USE THIS BOOK

What you are holding in your hands is yours to use as you wish. You may enjoy choosing a daily reading at random or you may want to read the same meditation each day for a week.

Or you can work your way straight through, if you feel adventurous, using this book to follow the Church calendar. Unfortunately, the enticing flow of the liturgical year, which developed over centuries, is not always immediately easy to appreciate. In the Church calendar feasts with fixed dates—such as Christmas and the Solemnity of Mary, Mother of God (January 1)—are interwoven with movable feasts such as the four Sundays in Advent and the Feast of the Epiphany. One fixed feast has a little movement: When the Feast of the Immaculate Conception (December 8) falls on Sunday, as it does in 1996, its celebration moves to Saturday.

The resulting calendar has several possible arrangements. The first three weeks of Advent are straightforward, interrupted only by the Feast of the Immaculate Conception. The fourth week of Advent is of variable length, for it ends on Christmas Eve. (The Jewish celebration of Hanukkah also occurs during this time of year; it can fall anywhere from late November to late December.)

Christmas Day is "the first day of Christmas" and

begins our counting of the familiar "Twelve Days of Christmas." There was a time when there were exactly twelve days from Christmas to Epiphany, January 6. But when Epiphany could occur on any day of the week, this great feast often passed neglected. And so, to assist us in celebrating it, the Church moved Epiphany from twelve days after Christmas to the Sunday immediately following New Year's Day. The Baptism of Our Lord, which brings our celebration of the Incarnation Season to a close and returns us to Ordinary Time, is the Sunday after Epiphany.

When Christmas does not fall on a Sunday, the order of the major feasts is Christmas, Feast of the Holy Family (Sunday), New Year's Day, Epiphany (Sunday) and the Baptism of the Lord (Sunday), with the lesser feasts, such as that of St. Stephen, filling in around these celebrations.

When Christmas is on a Sunday, then the Sunday sequence is Christmas, New Year's Day, Epiphany and Baptism of Our Lord, with the Holy Family feast omitted.

The chart on page 4 attempts to simplify all this confusion. There are sufficient meditations in this volume to accommodate all years. Therefore you will not always need all of the readings for Advent or for the days between Christmas and the Baptism.

However you choose to use this book, may you enjoy a grace-filled Incarnation Season!

Incarnation Season Dates

	1992	1993	1994
First Sunday of Advent	11/29	11/28	11/27
Second Sunday of Advent	12/6	12/5	12/4
Immaculate Conception	12/8	12/8	12/8
Third Sunday of Advent	12/13	12/12	12/11
Fourth Sunday of Advent	12/20	12/19	12/18
Christmas	12/25	12/25	12/25
Holy Family	12/27	12/26	—
Mary, Mother of God	1/1*	1/1*	1/1*
Epiphany	1/3*	1/2*	1/8*
Baptism of the Lord	1/10*	1/9*	1/15*
Hanukkah	12/20	12/9	11/28

* Of the new year.

1995	1996	1997	1998	1999
12/3	12/1	11/30	11/29	11/28
12/10	12/8	12/7	12/6	12/5
12/8	12/7	12/8	12/8	12/8
12/17	12/15	12/14	12/13	12/12
12/24	12/22	12/21	12/20	12/19
12/25	12/25	12/25	12/25	12/25
12/31	12/29	12/28	12/27	12/26
1/1*	1/1*	1/1*	1/1*	1/1*
1/7*	1/5*	1/4*	1/3*	1/2*
1/14*	1/12*	1/11*	1/10*	1/9*
12/18	12/6	12/24	12/14	12/4

Advent

A Time of Beginnings

appy New Year! Today, the first day of Advent,
we begin our Christian liturgical year. Of
course, our calendar year doesn't begin until
January 1—a legacy from the ancient Romans. They
named January after the Roman god, Janus, who had
two faces that looked in opposite directions—to the
past and to the future.

We Christians, however, are called to be like that
ancient Roman god. With our feet firmly planted in the
present, we look to the past. We look to our roots in
Judaism, to the historic Christ and his teachings, to
the faithful and heroic women and men who have
preceded us in our journeyings in time. It is our past
that gives us the privilege of celebrating liturgy; it is in
our remembrance of the past that the secret of our
redemption lies. We are to be a community of
memory.

And, with our feet still firmly planted in today, we
look to the future. We look ahead to this entire
Incarnation season and its celebration; we look to the
observance of this just-beginning liturgical year and
all the promises within it. We look to creation
becoming what it was meant to be; we look—and
work—to the bringing of God's reign upon earth. We
look to the coming of the cosmic Christ at the end of
this thing called time. We are called to be a forward-

looking, prophetic community.

Remembering and anticipating are important to us as Christians. And yet, we are to do both with our feet still planted firmly in today; we look to today in our recognition of Christ's existence in each other and in ourselves. We are to be a community of presence.

Many of the Scriptures chosen for the Incarnation Season specifically address one or more of these time references. As we listen carefully, quietly, receptively, we ask that the Holy Spirit help us balance yesterday, today and tomorrow in our lives.

CONSIDER:

♦ Where am I in my thoughts—yesterday, today, tomorrow?

♦ How do yesterday and tomorrow influence what I do today?

♦ How can *this* Incarnation Season help me keep yesterday, today and tomorrow balanced in my life?

A Time of Counting Down

U sually it begins the day after Thanksgiving. We are informed, reminded, even haunted by the ever-decreasing number of shopping days until Christmas. Should we by some miracle escape the blitz-tactics of the communications people, our kids perform the same service admirably. And we probably have our own countdowns: gifts to buy, wrap, send; cards to address and mail; events to attend. We are not allowed to forget!

Quite possibly we are counting down for a full month. That's a twelfth of the year! For all that time, our focus is on Christmas and all the ways in which Christmas touches our lives.

But, as we anticipate this yearly event, we may be overlooking one of the most important Christmas lessons of all. For when the Son of God stretched out his foot and stepped upon the earth as one of us, he exalted our own humanity; when Christ lived within the confines of time, he sanctified *our* time.

And so each day on earth is a gift, a most wonderful gift, from God. Life—our very existence—is a marvelous blessing from our Creator. How unfortunate that we should get so preoccupied in looking ahead that we forget the wonder of this moment, this instant, *now*!

The celebration of *now* requires practice and concentration. It takes the ability to "be still and know that I am God" (Psalm 46:10a, NRSV). It requires the ability to be aware of our own existence. How easy to become so absorbed in our preparations for the celebration of the historical Christ's birth that we completely ignore Christ present here, now. Christ is here. Christ is within us. Let us celebrate! Now!

CONSIDER:

♦ Why is it so difficult to celebrate the *now*?

♦ How does our culture help our celebration of the *now*? How does our culture hinder it?

♦ What one thing could I do to make myself more conscious of the present moment? How can I, even when I am busy, enjoy this day?

♦ What would I have to change around me in order to see each day as a special gift from God? What would I have to change within me in order to enjoy *now*?

A Time of Isaiah

The most familiar sections of the Hebrew Scriptures, or Old Testament, are the Book of Psalms, the stories from Genesis and verses from the Book of Isaiah. Isaiah is quoted from or referred to more than three hundred times in the New Testament!

Although the book is called Isaiah, only part of the first section was written by Isaiah of Jerusalem (Isaiah

1—39). The other two sections, usually referred to as Second Isaiah (Isaiah 40—55) and Third Isaiah (Isaiah 56—66), have unknown authors.

The Book of Isaiah covers significant times in the history of the Jewish people: preexilic, exilic, postexilic. Thus the Book of Isaiah begins before the Babylonian exile, covers the time of the exile itself and concludes with the resettlement following the return from exile. We miss these historical settings of First, Second and Third Isaiah if we allow our familiarity with the book to be limited to the sections quoted in liturgy. Some of the power of Isaiah is the continuing value of passages which, while pertinent to the specific time in which they were said or written, express insights and hope and faith that remain applicable for us today.

Here are a few Incarnation quotes from Isaiah:

> A voice cries out: In the desert prepare the way of the LORD! (40:3a)
>
> [T]he virgin shall be with child, and bear a son, and shall name him Immanuel. (7:14b)
>
> The people who walked in darkness
>   have seen a great light. (9:1a)
>
> Then the wolf shall be a guest of the lamb,
>   and the leopard shall lie down with the kid;
> The calf and the young lion shall browse together,
>   with a little child to guide them. (11:6)
>
> For a child is born to us, a son is given us;
>   upon his shoulder dominion rests.
> They name him Wonder-Counselor, God-Hero,
>   Father-Forever, Prince of Peace. (9:5)
>
> They shall beat their swords into plowshares
>   and their spears into pruning hooks.... (2:4b)

CONSIDER:

♦ What does each of the above verses say to me?

♦ What are other familiar Isaiah verses?

♦ What are my favorite quotes from Isaiah?

A Time of Stories

A wise rabbi once said, "God loves stories. That's why God created humanity."

The book which we refer to as "the Word of God" is not a theological dissertation, not a treatise on cosmology or ontology or any other "ology." The Creator did not need to issue such theological proclamations, for God could be confident that humanity would more than make up for any lack of such items.

No, God gave us a collection of short stories full of suspense, conflict, tragedy and apparent tragedy, and eventual triumph. And these stories, in turn, are all part of one great story—salvation history. At the end of time, when this largest book ever written is completed, the subtitle will be *The Love Affair Between God and Humanity*.

There is only *one* story, one indivisible whole. It includes the narrative of Christ's birth and also his death. It includes his parables and also the tribulations of the early Church. It includes today and the life of everyone here on earth now.

Christ's birth has meaning for us only because his death has meaning for us. And his death is remembered because of what happened after his death.

There is only *one* story. Advent, Christmas, Epiphany are celebrated only because we also celebrate Good Friday and Easter. The Incarnation has significance only because the Easter Triduum (Holy Thursday, Good Friday and Easter) has significance!

CONSIDER:

♦ What one word best describes my life story: for example, joyful, boring, inspiring, unselfish, fearful, courageous, faithful?

♦ Do I ever feel a part of a larger story? If yes, when? If no, why?

♦ Do I see myself as playing a unique role in the story of salvation history? When? Why or why not?

A Time of *Maranatha!*

Some words just can't be translated into other languages without something important being lost in the translation. When that happens, we often choose not to translate that word, but retain it even if we are speaking or writing a different language.

That's what has happened to *amen, hosanna, alleluia, maranatha.* In Paul's First Letter to the Corinthians (16:22) he used the Aramaic exclamation *maranatha,* assuming that people knew its meaning (it was probably used in the liturgies of that time).

When the New Testament was being written in Greek, *maranatha* was retained, both in Corinthians and in Revelation 22:20b, with the hope that it would express more eloquently the pent-up yearning of the community. Depending upon how the word is divided, it can mean "The Lord comes" (*maran'atha'*), or "Come, Lord!" (*marana'tha'*). There is a special beauty in the ambiguity of meanings: It is both proclamation and plea; it is both praise and petition; it is an excellent example of the self-fulfilled prophecy.

Maranatha! We say it in anticipation of our celebration of Christ's birth at Christmas. *Maranatha!* We say it in declaring Christ's presence among us and in us here and now. *Maranatha!* We say it with the evangelist John in our anticipation of Christ's Second Coming—the Parousia. Christ is forever coming!

CONSIDER:

♦ In what ways do I recognize the reality of the historical Christ?

♦ How real to me is the Christ present in those around me? How real to me is the Christ present within me? What impact does Christ have on my life?

♦ How real to me is the Christ of the Second Coming, the cosmic Christ?

A Time of Planning
Christmas Celebrations

We have difficulty celebrating! Granted that no one could ever accuse us of inability to plan the *activities* of a celebration, for we, as a society, excel at all the busyness involved in anticipating and preparing happenings. But is our celebration of Christmas confined to busyness— events wrapped in the trappings of the season?

One of the most popular and possibly too-familiar songs of the season is "The Twelve Days of Christmas." Those twelve days are the days between Christmas and the traditional date of Epiphany, January 6. That's when people used to celebrate— beginning with the first day of Christmas, Christmas Day. Before that was the season of Advent, a time of preparation, not a time for celebration.

But now the day after Christmas finds discarded Christmas trees tossed on rubbish heaps; the card shops begin displaying red lace hearts; the radio stations that previously played continuous Christmas music stopped at the stroke of midnight on the holy day; the TV channels cease holiday programming as if a time warp has occurred and Christmas is aeons in the past. There is a feeling that our world is attempting to wipe away all traces of the day.

We have lost contact with the integrity of the Advent-Christmas-Epiphany cycle. We, as a society, have also forgotten that celebration has several facets beyond activity. We've forgotten that celebration includes the less-than-strenuous "activities" of resting and meditating and remembering.

As we organize our activities of the Incarnation Season, let us recall that unity of the Advent-Christmas-Epiphany cycle. Let us also include in our plans both the time and the space for quiet celebrations even as we glory in the reason for our busyness. We can plan time for remembering and for "wasting time" in worship, in the quiet company of friends, in listening to music or in being content within ourselves as we enjoy both the day and the season.

So let us leave space on the calendar for looking at the Christmas cards (alone or with others) and reading *all* the texts; for telling family stories; for having a simple family/friends sing-a-long and singing *all* the verses of our favorite carols; for sitting quietly and looking at the Christmas tree and the decorations—the handmade ornaments, the ornaments that were gifts, those made by children, the ornaments that are family heirlooms.

Let us include on our calendar time to take delight in what we have done, in what Christ has done, in what Christ will do and in the world around us. Like God after creation or a woman after giving birth, we are to rest and rejoice in the miracle of life, both human and divine. Let's celebrate the fact that we exist and God exists! Only then can we touch the life-giving mystery that lies at the heart of the Incarnation.

CONSIDER:

♦ What are my expectations of Christmas Day?

♦ How can I help extend the feelings of celebration past the one day?

♦ How might I rewrite the text to "The Twelve Days of Christmas"?

♦ What can I do now to prepare to relax and enjoy the Incarnation Season?

A Time of Kind Words

The Talmud, the collection of Jewish law and tradition, states: "Whoever gives a small coin to a poor person receives six blessings, but one who speaks a kind word to that person receives eleven blessings." Being on the receiving end of kind words is always enjoyable; those words can make our hearts smile and our days more pleasant.

But to the poor, to those in need, to those who have been forced to "beg" in the ways our complicated society has invented, kind words can be much more than merely pleasant. They can be life-giving! Kind words can help build self-esteem, restore both honor and humor, provide purpose in life and affirm the essential dignity of all human beings.

An added bonus about kind words is that when we speak them, we too are blessed by the words we address to others.

This is the season of giving. We are besieged for funds from organizations familiar and unknown; street-corners have resident bell-ringers with kettles; the mail contains appeals for causes we never knew even existed; radio and TV celebrities try their effectiveness at talking us into giving.

As we respond with our coins and checks, let us remember the words of the Talmud. Those in need are deserving of our kind words; those making the appeals are also deserving.

CONSIDER:

♦ When have I been in need: financially, emotionally, spiritually? How important to me then were kind words?

♦ How does our society respond to people in need?

♦ What kind of need gets the most support? The least?

♦ When do I encounter people in need? How can my kind words assist them?

A Time of Preparation

There are some saints whose personal appeal and charisma continue to draw us to them. Despite years and distance, their stirring stories and miraculous legends continue to be told. Statues of St. Francis with his birds occupy honored spots in many gardens; St. Valentine's Day and St. Patrick's Day are celebrated by both non-Catholics and non-Christians; St. Nicholas has been so popular that he has been secularized into Santa Claus. But John the Baptist enjoys no such warm popularity!

The typical artistic representation of John is not appealing. His asceticism is portrayed by his bony build; his zealousness mirrored in the eyes of the fanatic; his angry rebelliousness etched on his countenance.

John was a transition person, the last of the Old Testament prophets, the first herald of the Good News. He was the humble forerunner who proclaimed "Here is your God!"

He also was the one crying "Repent!"—and his voice reaches to us over the centuries, for we, too, are called to repentance. But the Greek word *metanoia*, which is translated "repentance," means more than sorrow or regret for the past. It means something very positive: a conversion or a change of heart. It is a call not to the sorrowing repentance of Lent but to the making of room in our lives for our God. Conversion means that our life-style, our very existence, is a witness to our expectation of the Lord's coming. We are called to prepare for the Messiah by an emptying of self. Like Mary, we are to empty ourselves so that there is room for our divine Guest. We are welcoming the Good News of Christ—the ever-new, ever-growing and challenging gospel.

CONSIDER:

♦ Who are some other saints with appealing characteristics?

♦ How do I react to the description of John the Baptist in Scripture?

♦ Are there John the Baptist types in my life? How do I respond to them?

A Time of Music

Can we imagine the Incarnation Season without music? Everywhere there are Christmas programs, sing-alongs, caroling parties, musicals and, of course, Christmas carols. We are surrounded by a collage of music—from inane media jingles to grand cathedral performances of Handel's *Messiah*.

In church we sing of longing for Christ's coming, in school we sing of longing for Santa's coming and in the marketplace we sing of longing for customers' coming. Our symbols and metaphors, priorities and values, are decidedly mixed—which probably describes quite accurately our range and variety of emotions: saccharine piety, arrogant commercialism, worry, unselfishness, sentimental romanticism, zealousness, anxiety, Christian love.

Yet no matter how much we may trivialize this season, music will remain an integral part of our celebration, for words alone are inadequate to encompass the immensity of the Incarnation event.

And so each year we play our instruments and sing our songs about Santa and reindeer and toys and love and the Christ Child. But we must each remind ourselves: I am free to sing the song I choose.

CONSIDER

♦ What are my favorite Christmas carols?

♦ What are some of this season's musical compositions that are especially meaningful to me? Why?

♦ If I were to write the words for a Christmas carol, what kind of carol would it be? What topic would I choose?

♦ What does "I am free to sing the song I choose" mean to me?

A Time of Sharing

It is common to take a distorted view of sharing. Typically, sharing connotes the haves magnanimously giving to the have-nots. And the have-nots, knowing their place in society and aware of what is expected of them, receive their gifts humbly and gratefully.

But to share completely first recognizes that both parties have something to give; sharing requires that each is open to receive from the other. What is really expected of us is that we (who are regarded by most of the world as the haves) recognize the dignity of the have-nots by acknowledging that in their very lack may be something *we* need. We are called to recognize that they have learned from their suffering and lack, that they may have learned something which we do not know.

The hungry have learned from their hunger; the poor have learned from their poverty; people with disabilities have learned from their disabilities; the lonely have learned from their loneliness. They have learned what can only be taught by hunger and poverty and disability and loneliness and need.

Not until we are open to the gifts that only the hungry can offer to us will we know how to share our bread with them. Not until we recognize that the poor have insights to offer to us will we know how to relieve their poverty. Not until we learn what the great life-instructors such as poverty and need have to teach can we come to understand fully what we are to learn from having.

♦ What is my innermost feeling about charitable giving?

♦ When I try to imagine myself as homeless or disabled or very poor, what would be the hardest aspect of that condition for me to accept? Why?

♦ What are some of the offerings that the "disadvantaged," those who live at the margins of society, have for me?

A Time of Shopping

O nce upon a time, there was a missionary living on a small island in the Pacific. At Christmas, a young man in the village presented the missionary with a seashell.

"This is a lovely shell—and it is perfect!" But then the missionary, looking more closely at the shell, recognized its rarity in the area of the village.

"My friend," he said, "these shells are found only on the far side of the island. You had to walk a very great distance to get this shell."

"Yes, Father," answered the boy. "But the long walk is part of the gift."

Included in the gifts under the Christmas tree will be long walks in department store aisles and long waits in check-out lines. Gifts both given and received will be accompanied by encounters with rude and unresponsive clerks, unpredictable shipping schedules, late mailings of back-order items, mislabeling and missing parts, all-thumbs gift-wrapping sessions. These are all part of the long walk for our various "seashells." Not only are they part of the gift, they may even be of more value than the gift itself. And we are grateful for all the long walks included in the gifts we receive.

CONSIDER:

♦ How do I determine the value of Christmas gifts I give? Their cost? The amount of effort expended? The amount of time?

♦ How do I evaluate the worth of gifts I receive? Amount of money spent? Creativity involved? Time expended?

♦ How do I feel about the "long walks" in my Christmas shopping?

A Time of Mary and Martha

Who said we had to be *either* a Mary or a Martha? Why is the question usually presented as an either/or choice? As Christians each one of us is called to be a unique combination of both! Mary and Martha represent the two extremes that exist in each of us. Martha is our busy and active self; Mary is our reflective, prayerful self. We are ever both.

Certainly we are called to be busy, for we are the hands and feet of God on this earth. Certainly we are called to prayer, for prayer is our relationship with God. Thus it is not busyness that is to be avoided, but rather busyness without purpose. It is not activity that is wrong, rather misdirected activity, or activity without thought. Nor, surely, is it prayer that is wrong.

As many saints have assured us through their words and lives, the busier we are, the greater our need of prayer. The busier we are, the greater our need for reflection; the more we have to do, the more important that each task brings us closer to God. The noisier the world around us, the more intently we must listen to the still small voice of God within each of us.

It is in prayer that we find the reasons for our busyness; it is through meditation and reflection that we find the direction for our activity.

Without prayer, reflection, meditation, how can we establish our priorities? Without prayer, reflection, meditation, how can we avoid discouragement? Without prayer, reflection, meditation, how can we discern the will of God?

CONSIDER:

- How do I handle being very busy? When am I at my best?

- When I am very busy, what are the first things I drop from my activities? Why?

- What is the difference between the busyness of a crisis, such as a serious illness or death in the family, and the busyness of everyday life?

- When do I feel most comfortable with the Mary/ Martha balance in my own life?

A Time of Darkness and Light

I t is the time of the year when we seek out light, for during the winter solstice, we experience the days of least daylight.

It is the time when we seek out the light of the prophets for, as Hildegard of Bingen said, "Prophets illuminate the darkness." Advent is a time of prophets, a time when we read from the writings of Isaiah, when we learn of John the Baptizer.

It is a time for candles—the candles of the Advent Wreath, the candles of table-centerpieces, the candles in our churches. The light of the Advent candles heralds the birth of Christ, who is the light of the world.

As Christmas nears, we see more and more lights. There are colored lights, flashing lights, twinkling lights, traveling lights; there are decorative lights on Christmas trees, on houses, in yards; there are light displays in stores and shopping malls and office buildings.

In the predawn darkness of Advent we look to all these sources of light. Yet they serve to remind us that *we* too are called to be prophets—prophets proclaiming God's reign, prophets announcing Christ's Second Coming. And, as Christ is the Light of the World, so too are we. For as Christ's followers, we are to bring his love to all humanity; we are to reflect the light of Christ; we, too, are to be the light of the world.

CONSIDER:

♦ What does light symbolize for me?

♦ What are some of the reasons that candles are used in so many religious celebrations and rituals?

♦ In the Northern Hemisphere Christmas occurs in winter, during the time of most darkness. In the Southern Hemisphere, however, Christmas occurs at the height of summer—during the days of longest daylight. How might darkness and light be considered symbolically there?

♦ Do I consider myself a prophet, a "light to the world"? How might I become more of a prophet and a light to the world?

A Time of Gifting

Sometimes we open a gift and it takes our breath away. We are not merely pleasantly surprised, we are astonished!

On occasion, this reaction may be due to the expensiveness of the gift. Or it is because of the extra "something" about the gift: It may eloquently express the love of the giver, the generosity of time of the giver, the creativity or inspiration of the giver.

How wonderful when our breath-taking reaction is because the gift-giver has chosen an item which expresses faith or trust in us. Then the gift becomes an affirmation of us! The gift reminds us of our talents and abilities, our uniqueness, our hopes for the future. The gift is a vote of confidence in us; the gift tells us we are appreciated and loved; the gift is a declaration of faith in us. And through that gift, we are truly blessed!

CONSIDER:

♦ What are some gifts I have received in the past that have been affirmations of faith in me?

♦ How have I reacted to a gift that expresses faith in me, in my ability, in my talents?

♦ How can I choose gifts for others that are affirmations of them as unique members of God's family?

♦ How does the gift of Christ fit into this description of a gift that overwhelms us? Affirms us?

A Time of the Magnificat

Today we celebrate not Christ's conception in Mary but Mary's conception in her mother, Anne. From that very first moment, Mary's soul was set apart, free of the entanglements that the rest of us experience.

On this wonderful Marian feast, the Church has chosen her song—the Magnificat (see page 118)—for the Responsorial Psalm of the day. Like all Responsorial Psalms, it is meant to be sung, for words alone cannot express the liveliness of Mary's praise.

This most marvelous of ancient canticles sums up the Hebrew Scriptures while it anticipates the gospel. The evangelist Luke gives us, through the Magnificat, a spiritual interpretation of the mystery of the Incarnation.

As Mary concentrates on praising God, she experiences simultaneously the fear and love, the attraction and awe that confrontation with the Holy produces. In God's presence she truly knows herself. While the Magnificat is a glorious hymn of praise, it is also a noble song of Mary's humility, for humility is, at its most basic level, honesty and truthfulness. Humility recognizes our limitations as human beings, yet also recognizes the munificent grandeur to which

God raises us. God blesses us, each and every one, with gifts. To refuse such gifts insults the divine Giver; to deny the presence of such gifts belittles our intelligence, our senses, our awareness as creatures of God.

In the fullness of joy Mary magnifies God for what God has done in her, has done for the world, has done for all history and time. In her exuberance she allows herself to be overtaken with prayerful spiritual inebriation. Mary is "high" on God!

Mary thus becomes the first Christian, the first follower of Christ. As such, she has been honored throughout history and was chosen at Vatican II as the model of the Church. Her Magnificat is the song we sing enthusiastically and with abandon when we allow ourselves to be as open to God as was Mary. Her Magnificat becomes the song of the entire Church; it is our song.

CONSIDER:

♦ How do I define *humility*?

♦ What does "high on God" mean to me?

♦ What would I include in my own Magnificat?

♦ What are my gifts which give praise to my Creator?

HANUKKAH

A Time of Kinship

The Jewish festival of Hanukkah, or Festival of
Lights, occurs during the Advent season. Since
it commemorates the Dedication of the Second
Temple in 165 B.C.E. (*Before the Common Era*), it
predates Christ. Mary, Joseph and Jesus probably
celebrated this festival in their home.

The history of the event is contained in Maccabees
1 and 2. The Syrians tried to convert the Jews to
Hellenism, the Greek religion. At first the attempts
had been subtle or only gently persuasive, but
eventually the Syrian ruler Antiochus decided that
Jews would no longer have a choice. He seized the
Temple and rededicated it as a temple to the Greek
god, Zeus.

The Jews, first under the leadership of Mattathias
and then his son Judas Maccabeus, fought the
Syrians. Although the Jews were greatly outnumbered
by the Syrians, they were successful in regaining the
Temple, which the Syrians had defiled. The Jews
cleaned out the Temple and rededicated it, restoring
the light that had always burned there. And, according
to Talmudic commentaries, although there was only
enough oil to keep the light burning for one day, the
oil lasted for eight days and nights.

The Jewish observance of Hanukkah celebrates
both the victory of Judas Maccabeus and the miracle

of the oil light. It is a joyous, family-centered, eight-day celebration, featuring the lighting of the *Hanukiyot*, the nine-cupped candelabra often called the Hanukkah menorah. One of the candle cups is removable. Called the *shamash*, the servant light, it is used to light the other candles. One candle is lit the first night, two the second, continuing until all eight are lit.

Central to the Hanukkah celebration are singing, gift-giving, eating *latkes* or potato pancakes, using oil in cooking, decorating and playing the dreidel game (a dreidel is a four-sided top).

CONSIDER:

♦ Christ grew up in a Jewish home and was educated in the Jewish faith. While he preached against some abuses of the day, other practices he retained. What are some Jewish beliefs and practices that he rejected? What are some he retained?

♦ When I reflect on my attitude toward the Jews, do I feel a special kinship toward these people with whom I share a common heritage? If yes, how and when? If no, why not?

A Time of Joy

The Church reminds us today to be joyful! In the pre-Vatican II liturgy this Sunday was called "Rose Sunday," for the day's liturgical color was rose, considered the color of joy. Today we use the phrase "looking through rose-colored glasses" to describe someone who seems to see only the good.

Yet, though it seems rather curious, most of us do have to be reminded to be joyful! Or, we need reminding about all the reasons we have to be joyful. The only people who don't need the reminder are saints—people who live so intimately in the love of God that they are ever enveloped in God's joy—even when walking to their martyrdom.

Such joy is not blindness to pain or sorrow or need. Rather, it is the recognition of the reality of God's love; it is the presence of the Holy Spirit within us; it is the realization that divine love is greater than any other force in the world. Christian joy is our response to the Good News.

Thus, it is possible to be joyful in the midst of the Christmas hassle; it is possible to be serenely joyful despite unfulfilled plans, unaccomplished "to-do" lists, limited budgets, Christmas tree lights that don't light and sore feet. Somehow, all these things become changed when viewed through those rose-colored glasses of God's love. It is God's will that we be joyful!

CONSIDER:

- Why should I be joyful?

- What is the difference between "having a good time" and being joyful?

- What does "Laughter is holy!" mean to me?

- When do I experience joy? When have I experienced joy despite pain or disappointment?

- Whom do I know who is a truly joyful person? What makes him/her joyful?

- What is the relationship between joy and faith?

A Time of Gifts

We are gifts. We are unique, wonderful gifts to each other. Each and every one of us is a one-time-only gift to the universe. We who are indeed "fearfully, wonderfully made" (Psalm 139:14b) are, quite literally, God's gift to the world!

What a humbling and, at the very same instant, exhilarating thought! How freeing—and yet how binding!

This is the time of the year when so much of our thoughts and efforts concern gifts, especially the gifts we buy or make for others. And, of course, we recognize Christ, who always was and always is and always shall be a gift to us. But it is also a good time to recall our own giftedness, to claim it gratefully, to use it wisely and unselfishly.

There are people in our lives for whom the most appreciated present is *our presence*! There are people in our lives for whom our words—written or spoken— are our most valuable gifts.

We *are*. And because we are, we are gifts of God to each other and to the world.

CONSIDER:

♦ Do I have a sense of being "a gift to the world"? If not, why not?

♦ Who of us has obligations to the world? Why?

♦ How do I claim my talents? How can I best use my talents? How can I best use my gift of presence?

A Time of Graciousness

"**H**ail, Mary, full of grace!" How overflowing with grace was Mary when she was pregnant with the God-Christ!

The words *graciousness* and *grace* come from the same root word: *gratia*, which means favor or grace. Although graciousness may be expressed in a sensitivity to details or to an awareness of others, it is much more than politeness or the use of proper etiquette. Graciousness goes far beyond the rules of Emily Post or the suggestions of Miss Manners. Graciousness springs forth from the presence of grace within us.

Graciousness can be expressed in our gift-giving. Graciousness is the ability to sense when a friend "needs" a gift; graciousness is able to give a gift in secret; graciousness senses when a gift should not be given in return for a present since the giver needs to experience the delightful joy of giving without repayment. Graciousness chooses gifts with the receiver—and not the giver—as the main concern.

A gracious person thus views Christmas-giving with the good of the receiver uppermost in thought, with no consideration of the cost to himself/herself. That's why we can say God is gracious—the original Christmas Gift has been given to us with no consideration of the cost to God! Advent is the time set aside to discover (or rediscover) the element of goodness and godliness—Christ—that is within us. Mary, filled with the womb-bound Christ, was gracious. We, filled with the sacrament of Christ, the spirit of Christ, are also to respond to that presence with our graciousness.

As creatures of a loving God, we are all called to have the life of the gracious God within us. At this busy, harried, emotional time, we are surrounded with opportunities to express this graciousness in our thoughts and words and actions. As we encounter one another on our errands, as we work beside each other, as we correspond with others, to each we can say in our thoughts, "The gracious Christ in me greets the Christ in you."

CONSIDER:

♦ What are some examples of graciousness I have observed in other people? What are some examples during this Incarnation Season?

♦ How can I be gracious in my gift-giving?

♦ How do I feel about receiving a gift and not giving one in return?

♦ Would anything change in the world if people greeted each other with "The gracious Christ in me greets the Christ in you"?

A Time of Blessing

Years ago, at some forgotten time, we Christians lost a treasure. Somewhere, without realizing what was happening, we allowed a beautiful and enriching ritual slip away through disuse. Somehow, we placed our "blessing privilege" in the category reserved for the ordained.

Perhaps this happened as a result of our tendency to divide the world into two separate entities—the sacred and the secular. It is time to recognize the sacredness of the ordinary; it is also time to reclaim our blessing privilege!

The Scriptures contain many instances of people who are not priests blessing others: Fathers blessed sons, parents blessed children, friends blessed friends. At the Visitation, when Mary visited Elizabeth, Elizabeth greeted the young mother-to-be with a blessing; at the Presentation in the Temple, Simeon blessed the Holy Family.

This is the season when we recognize that God uniquely blessed humanity by becoming one of us. It is also an appropriate time for us to reclaim our heritage: Our vocation is to bless! As the People of God, as people called to be holy, we are intended to bless—to bless each other, to bless the universe in which we have been created.

When we bless another, we give praise and thanks to God for both that person and for ourself. When we bless another, we are extending ourself to the person being blessed, and we symbolize this by touching the person or extending our hands over the person. And in so doing, both the blesser and the blessee are blessed. For blessing is always a cyclic occurrence; as we bless, so we are blessed. The psalmist understood this when he wrote: "Bless the LORD, O my soul!" (Psalm 103:1a; 104:1a).

CONSIDER:

♦ What do I see as the difference between blessing a person and praying for that person?

♦ Have I ever been blessed by another person other than a priest or minister? What were the circumstances? What were my reactions?

♦ Have I ever blessed another person? How did I feel about doing it? How do I feel about blessing *things*?

♦ What prevents me from becoming a "blessing person"?

A Time of Silence

I t is in the silence that God speaks to us. Elijah learned this long ago (see 1 Kings 19). Having been told that the Lord would be passing by, Elijah stood on the mountain, waiting. A wind, powerful enough to crush rocks, roared past the mountain; an earthquake violently shook the ground;

a fire raged through the area. But God was not in the wind or the earthquake or the fire. After all the noise and chaos, there came a soft, whispering sound, and there was God.

Often God uses the wind or earthquake or fire to get our attention. But it is only in the silence that we hear the soft, whispering divine voice.

Silence is not just the absence of noise, for silence's communication goes beyond hearing. We must see silence; touch it; have the awesome boldness to enter into the silence—for that's where God is.

Silence is an integral part of our Advent preparation, for only in this silence can we prepare properly for the presence of Christ.

Silence is an integral part of our Incarnation celebration, for only in this silence can we acknowledge properly the presence of Christ.

It is in this silence that we are and God is. It is here that we encounter mystery: the mystery of God, the mystery of ourselves, the mystery of others. This silence is celebration in its most elemental sense.

CONSIDER:

♦ What is my reaction to silence? Why?

♦ How can silence be part of preparation? Part of celebration?

♦ Is silence part of my day? My week? My life?

A Time of Panic

The deadline is rapidly approaching! As it bears down on us unrelentingly, we may find ourselves nearing panic. Our focus flits from one thing to another as we become obsessed with crossing the item-of-the-moment off our list! Our original spending guide is ignored as we concentrate on buying *something* for that person. Or we want to get a tree, any tree!

Panic rarely travels alone. It is usually accompanied by Fatigue, Discouragement, Depression.

When Panic begins peering around the corner at us, it is time to reestablish our priorities. It is amazing to realize how unimportant so many anxieties become when placed in the context of salvation history!

It is time to recall that the Incarnation is a season—not just one day. Therefore, the gifts received after Christmas Day are not only welcomed but also are still timely; the cards and letters received then are read more leisurely; cookies and other goodies are appreciated even more later in the year. And if the flight home is delayed because of weather, it is a disappointment but not a catastrophe.

The "real" Christmas story is full of details that somehow must have seemed less than ideal to the participants. Had Mary experienced a moment of panic at Gabriel's visit? Had Joseph felt panic-stricken at the news of Mary's pregnancy? Surely Mary did not want to be separated from family and friends at such an important time as the birth of her baby. Joseph must have grieved that his wife, without the traditional support of her family or friends, had to give birth in a stable. And that flight into Egypt certainly was not how they had planned to begin their lives as new parents.

And yet, in spite of all these panic-producing situations, God did become incarnate. In the context of salvation history, that is what is important and overpowering, consoling and challenging, unbelievable and faith-building, affirming and subduing, sustaining and joyous, fulfilling and....

CONSIDER:

♦ What would "ruin" Christmas for me?

♦ What do I enjoy the most during the Incarnation Season?

♦ What means do I use to prevent panic at this time?

♦ What means do I use to reestablish realistic expectations in my holiday activities?

A Time of Matthew

"**K**now your audience" is an often-repeated bit of advice to writers. When Matthew began writing his Gospel, he knew his audience and directed his words to them. Matthew wrote for Jews familiar with the Scriptures, Jews who knew the prophesies concerning the coming of the Messiah, Jews anxiously awaiting that Messiah. That is why he began his Gospel with a lengthy description of the lineage of Jesus, for this would be important to the Jews. While we today may be bored by that long list of names, the Jews of Matthew's day were most interested in it. Matthew, anxious that the Jews recognize and accept Christ as the Messiah, pointed out Jesus' Davidic lineage through Joseph, Mary's husband.

Matthew compares Christ to Moses to illustrate that Christ is the new Moses who has come to fulfill the Law. It is in Matthew's Gospel that Christ is often addressed with the Jewish title *rabbi*, which means "teacher."

Although Matthew was writing for Jewish Christians, he knew that Christ had come to all peoples. And so he included in his Infancy Narratives the visit of the Magi to illustrate Christ's mission to the entire world. The Magi had been led to Christ by a star, the symbol of faith. The Magi themselves, who were not Jewish, represented the Gentiles, to whom Christ also came.

♦ If I were writing a Gospel now, who would my audience be? What would I consider important to include?

♦ What would I include to convince the people I know of the importance of Christ's teachings?

♦ How would I go about proving to my audience Christ's divinity?

FOURTH SUNDAY OF ADVENT

A Time of Children

As the world is being readied for the Messiah, our Scripture readings have focused upon the adult Christ who will come again. Only now, on this last Sunday of Advent, do we read about Mary and Joseph and the approaching birth of the divine Child.

When all the theologizing is completed, all the sophisticated interpretations are silenced, what remains is quite simple: God comes to us as a baby, a child.

And so this time belongs to children. And we adults, distracted by the complications of life in which we manage to immerse ourselves, are to turn to children to receive the message God gives to us through them.

It is children who regard all of life as mystery; it is children whose universe is play and whose play is their work; it is children who recognize that the commonplace remains ever miraculous while accepting the occurrence of miracles as ordinary acts of the God who loves us.

It is children who recall to us our imagination and exuberance and creativity; it is children who excel us in natural wisdom; it is children who understand the spirit of the law, refusing to become obsessed with its letter.

It is children who most openly express their need

for love, their unquestioning acceptance of love, their spontaneous giving of love.

To children we say, "Welcome, little ones! Thank you for all you teach us!"

CONSIDER:

♦ What does "Become like children" (Matthew 18:1-5) mean to me?

♦ What does "A little child shall guide them" (Isaiah 11:6) mean to me?

♦ How does my relationship to the infant Christ differ from my relationship to the adult Christ?

A Time of Expectation

We are waiting. During this time before Christmas, we pause in our managing of life, and wait.

Our waiting is not idleness and boredom but joyful expectation and excited anticipation of what is to come. This pre-Christmas time is creative in the deepest, most wonderful and profound sense. During Advent we are all like Mary! We are all pregnant with the Christ Child. And Christ, too, waits. Christ is waiting to be born within us, to have a deeper relationship with us, to be with us always.

We wait. And we surround ourselves with the color of waiting, dark blue-violet. Blue has long been considered Mary's color and we are waiting as did Mary. Dark blue-violet is also the color of the predawn sky. It was into the darkness of the Jewish world of defeat and occupation that the light of the Messiah came so long ago. It is against that dark blue-violet backdrop that we await the dawn when the Christ-light shall shine so that all can see.

We wait. We shall be able to participate actively in our celebration of the Incarnation only if we now allow ourselves to participate passively and meditatively. This is a time of self-emptying, of waiting on Christ's grace, of attending carefully to what Christ is asking of us.

CONSIDER:

♦ Why is waiting so difficult?

♦ How do I imagine Mary waiting?

♦ What am I waiting for in my life? How does this affect what I do now?

♦ What are my expectations of Christmas? Of the Incarnation Season? Is a closer relationship with God one of my expectations of this season? Of anytime in the future?

A Time of Faith

J oseph is the strong, silent male lead in the
Incarnation narrative. Mary's words are recorded
for us in a number of places in Scripture. John the
Baptist has his say. So do his parents, Elizabeth
and Zechariah. The angels speak and sing. We hear
from the Magi, King Herod, Simeon—but not Joseph.

Scripture does not record Joseph's reply at his
angelic annunciation, but we are told that Joseph took
Mary for his wife. Scripture does not record Joseph's
response to the angelic warning of danger to the
family, but we know that Joseph took Mary and the
Babe to the safety of Egypt.

In the Jewish tradition it is the male who has the
obligation to pray. Yet for centuries, artists have
presented to us Mary at prayer, but not Joseph. Joseph
always seems to be busy—leading the Mary-carrying
donkey to Bethlehem, seeking shelter there, working
in his carpentry shop.

From that extremely patriarchal society, no words
of Joseph's are recorded, just deeds. No prayers or
statements of faith are given, just deeds of faith. And,
though Joseph evidently lived long enough that
during Christ's preaching days, Christ was referred to
as "the carpenter's son," still we find no recorded
words of Joseph's, only his trade, his deeds.

Joseph may be a shadowy figure in salvation
history, but one thing is certain: He was a man of faith.

- ♦ What do I imagine Joseph saying to Mary and Jesus in Bethlehem? In Egypt? In Nazareth?

- ♦ How do I picture Joseph? What does this say about my concept of the Holy Family?

- ♦ Who in my circle of family or friends most exemplifies the quiet faith of Joseph? How can I express my gratitude for the example of that person's faithfulness?

A Time of the Infancy Narratives

I *nfancy Narratives* is the term referring to those very familiar sections of Luke and Matthew which tell of the birth of Christ.

Though our celebration of the Nativity is an integral and important part of Christianity, the Infancy Narratives themselves form a quite small part of the New Testament. The events surrounding Christ's birth are contained in only four chapters (Matthew 1—2; Luke 1—2) out of the entire four Gospels. Mark and John tell us nothing concerning Christ's birth.

Like so much of Scripture, the Infancy Narratives were written years after the events described. In fact, they were written long after the Resurrection story, for only then did people realize the importance of Christ's life and his birth. And it was not until the fourth century that Christians began to celebrate Christmas. Since no one knew the actual date of Christ's birth, Christmas was placed on the calendar to compete with the pagan feast of the "unconquered Sun God" in Rome. It seemed appropriate to choose December 25 to celebrate the birth of the unconquered Son of God!

But this history does not diminish for us the truth of the Infancy Narratives. Facts can be barriers for us in our search for truth. Superfluous details, distracting peripheral action, conflicting accounts can pull our attention away from truth. Facts speak only to the head; truth speaks to head and heart and soul. Our belief in God's word is not dependent upon verification by historians as to date and place and time, for spiritual truth may not coincide with historical truth.

Instead, as we read Scripture we are overwhelmed with the sheer weight of the evidence of God's continuing love affair with us.

CONSIDER:

♦ What are some of the different ways I can read Scripture?

♦ How can I read it as poetry, responding to its imagery and appreciating the beauty of the language?

♦ How can I read it as a story, looking for recurring themes and repeated truths?

◆ How do I resolve apparent conflicts between Scripture and history or Scripture and science?

A Time of Luke

L uke is the gentle, sensitive, articulate, educated Greek physician. It is to Luke as Gospel writer that we owe our gratitude for most of the details of Christ's Incarnation. It is only in Luke's Gospel that we learn of Zechariah and Elizabeth and the birth of their son John, who became known as the Baptizer; of the angel Gabriel's annunciation to Mary; of Mary's visit to Elizabeth; of Mary's and Joseph's trip to Bethlehem and Christ's birth in a stable there; of the shepherds and the angels; of the circumcision, the presentation in the Temple and the finding of the young Christ in the Temple.

Luke gives us the texts of the great Incarnation canticles or songs: Zechariah's Canticle ("Blessed be the Lord, the God of Israel..."; 1:68a), the *Magnificat* of Mary (1:46b-55), the *Gloria* of the angels (2:14) and the *Nunc Dimittis* of Simeon ("Now, Master, you may let your servant go in peace..."; 2:29a).

Unfortunately, as we wrap the Incarnation story in sentimentality and surround it with kid-appeal, we may also succeed in disguising the radicalism of Luke's Gospel. For example, though Christ—and Luke—lived in a patriarchal society, Mary is the dominant family figure in Luke's account. He describes to us Mary's annunciation rather than Joseph's, which Matthew notes. Throughout Luke's account of Christ's life women played important roles, and he repeatedly gives equal time to them: At the presentation in the Temple we learn not only of Simeon, but also of Anna, the prophet; the parable of the shepherd and the lost sheep is balanced with the parable of the woman and the lost coin. Luke gives us a Savior identified with the poor, the outcast, the handicapped, the criminal. In the society of Christ's time no one was considered more undesirable than a Samaritan, yet Luke tells us the parable of the Good Samaritan and the story of the grateful Samaritan cured of leprosy.

In the gentle, familiar flow of Luke's Gospel we must not lose our own sensitivity to the radical challenges of the gospel message.

CONSIDER:

♦ What mental image of Luke, the man, do I get from reading his Gospel?

♦ In my familiarity with the Incarnation story, have I lost touch with its radicalism?

♦ If the Messiah came today, in this culture, where might he/she be born? How might the radicalism of the Messiah be expressed today?

A Time for the 'O Antiphons'

The "O Antiphons" (see page 132) are recited or sung during Evening Prayer (Vespers) of the Liturgy of the Hours for seven days before Christmas, from December 17 to December 23. They are the Church's final effort at preparing for Christmas.

Each antiphon begins with the interjection "O": O Wisdom; O Lord; O Root of Jesse; O Key of David; O Rising Sun; O King of Nations; O Emmanuel.

Each of these antiphons presents us with one or more Old Testament figures or types, which were understood by the early Church as referring to Christ. Christ was the Wisdom active in creation, the "Covenant of God"—Adonai—of the Chosen People, of the root or lineage of Jesse as a descendant of David. The key of David was a sign of the promised redeemer. Christ is the rising sun, the light eternal, the sun of justice. Active among the Gentiles, he is therefore King of Nations. And, finally, God with us—Emmanuel—is Christ.

These antiphons form the basis for the familiar Advent hymn "O Come, O Come, Emmanuel," in which each verse addresses Christ under a different title.

The poetic prayers of the "O Antiphons" express both the expectancy and the longing of the Hebrew people for the Messiah. The Jews, wishing they knew God's timetable, longed to be able to count the days until the coming of the Messiah who, they believed, would free them from bondage.

Today we pray the "O Antiphons" to express our expectancy and longing for a closer union with God and our awaiting of Christ's Second Coming.

CONSIDER:

♦ Which is my favorite "O Antiphon" title for Christ? Why?

♦ Do I ever experience this deep longing for a closer union with God? If yes, when? If no, why?

♦ Is there anything I can do to bring about a closer union with God? Am I willing to do whatever that is?

A Time of 'Yes!'

L et us imagine for a moment that Mary's was not the first name on the Archangel Gabriel's list of prospective mothers for the Son of God. Suppose, for example, that a number of other young women had been offered the opportunity. But when Gabriel could offer no guarantee of pain-free success, no project plan or outline, no written warranty, the candidates all answered, "Thanks, but no thanks," to the archangel's offer.

Gabriel may have arrived at the home of Mary, betrothed to Joseph, carpenter, quite flustered from crisscrossing the Promised Land visiting Jewish maidens. The scenario may even have been a bit ragged. "Hail—" (Gabriel pauses to consult his list) "Mary." But he does get his message delivered and, praise God, she says yes. And the miracle begins.

If we cannot imagine Mary's no, then her yes has no meaning. But getting back to our story—it might be thought that in this product of our fanciful imagination, God would seem to be settling for second best. But such would not be the case, for it would be precisely Mary's willingness that immediately placed her first among the candidates; it would be the yes that marked her above all others.

God presents us all with opportunities in many different ways. Occasionally God does hit us over the head to get our attention; occasionally someone is struck off his or her high horse on the way to Damascus, Detroit or downtown.

But more often our "annunciation" comes as the soft touch of an angel wing, a zephyr whisper of an angelic voice, the brief passing of a heavenly visitor. The question comes unencumbered with guarantees, free of packaging paraphernalia. It comes as a bare and simple question. It comes as a need of the world.

And just as often the question is asked of those who, in the estimation of the worldly-wise, are not the first choice; they may appear ill-prepared for the challenges ahead. And yet, it is at the instant of saying yes that their qualifications become apparent. They are willing!

In our own lives the question can take on many forms. However it appears or is asked of us, it remains an idea without flesh until our yes—our leap of faith, our courageous, foolish, astounding, humbling

recognition that God is asking *us*!
And the miracle begins.

♦ What is God asking of me now, today, that I prefer
to ignore?

♦ How long has it been since I have felt challenged,
stretched, tested?

♦ How might I be trying to avoid spiritual, emotional,
intellectual, psychological growth?

♦ Have I filled my life with so much noisy activity that
I no longer can hear the still, small voice within me?

Christmas

CHRISTMAS DAY

(December 25)

Celebrating Love

J oyful, joyful! This is the day we celebrate God's humanization and our divinization! This is the day we celebrate love!

But love is not always predictable or easily defined. And, contrary to what Paul says in his often-quoted First Letter to the Corinthians, love is not always the unemotional, patient, strictly controlled force described there (see 1 Corinthians 13:1-8a).

Yes, love is kind and not self-seeking; but love is also drawn to excess, extravagance, exuberance. Love is characterized by impatience to be with the loved one, by an excessive willingness to sacrifice for the good of the other, by an exuberant delight in the other. Love is characterized by *passion*.

Today we celebrate the excessive, extravagant exuberance of God's love for us. Today we celebrate God's yearning for human intimacy, which could be fulfilled only by becoming one of us. Today we celebrate the expansive, limitless, consuming fire of God's love.

The Incarnation—God's coming to earth as one of us—is the act of a *passionate* Lover!

CONSIDER:

♦ In what ways do I think of God's love for us as being similar to human love?

♦ In what ways do I think of God's love for us as being different from human love?

♦ How is my love for God similar to my love for another human being? How does it differ?

FEAST OF ST. STEPHEN

(December 26)

Celebrating the Gospel's Challenge

O nly if we have prepared for an adult Christ coming at Christmas, only if we have looked at the radicalism of his gospel, only if we have accepted the challenges of being Christian—only then can we possibly understand and accept what the Church is telling us today in our celebration of the Feast of St. Stephen.

Here we are, the day after Christmas. Amid the holiday trappings, with Christmas lullabies playing in the background, we exchange the red of Santa's outfit and Rudolph's nose for the red of martyrs' blood! Stephen, whose story comes to us in the Acts of the Apostles, is a dedicated convert to the new religion; he is the first of the "seven" chosen by the apostles to serve the poor. Stephen becomes the first of an unknown number of people throughout time to be martyred for being a Christian.

Christ did not come into this world to be confined to a sentimental story told yearly to children. Christ did not come so that we could be enveloped in an annual frenzy of tinsel and cards and cookies. Christ came to teach us to love—and the price of love may be a martyr's death. This is what the Church is reminding us today. Christian love, as Christ defined and lived

love, may exact a terrible price in tears and blood and
anguish.

CONSIDER:

♦ How do I define love? How did Christ define or
describe love?

♦ How do I feel about celebrating this feast the day
after Christmas?

♦ Whom do I know who is a martyr for his or her
beliefs?

Celebrating the Word

B racketed between the commemorations of
martyred Stephen and the Holy Innocents is
this celebration of John the Evangelist.
Perhaps the Church is reminding us between the
slaughters that it is love that is important.

Although John did not write any Infancy Narratives
as such, he wrote some of the most beautiful poetry
ever written about Christ's birth. For centuries this
was read, in Latin, as the "Last Gospel" at every Mass:

> In the beginning was the Word,
>   and the Word was with God,
>   and the Word was God.
> He was in the beginning with God.
> All things came to be through him,
>   and without him nothing came to be.
> What came to be through him was life,
>   and this life was the light of the human race;
> the light shines in the darkness,
>   and the darkness has not overcome it.

A man named John was sent from God. He came for
testimony, to testify to the light, so that all might
believe through him. He was not the light but came to
testify to the light. The true light, which enlightens
everyone, was coming into the world.

He was in the world,
    and the world came to be through him,
    but the world did not know him.
He came to what was his own,
    but his own people did not accept him.

But to those who did accept him he gave power to
become children of God, to those who believe in his
name, who were born not by natural generation nor by
human choice nor by a man's decision but of God.

    And the Word became flesh
        and made his dwelling among us,
        and we saw his glory,
        the glory of the Father's only Son,
        full of grace and truth. (John 1:1-14)

CONSIDER:

♦ What are some of the poetic ways in which I refer to
  God: for example, Word, Light, Wind, Mystery,
  Womb, Fire, Love, Existence?

♦ What are the most meaningful ways in which I
  relate to God: for example, as the Trinity, the
  human-divine Christ, the Creator, the Holy Spirit?

♦ What are the advantages of thinking of God in such
  terms? The disadvantages?

Celebrating the Life-Death Journey

Death again! Martyrdom of innocent babies! How do we celebrate this feast? Can we grieve and rejoice simultaneously? In fact, that is exactly what we as Christians are called to do!

From the very first Christmas, death is inevitably involved in the Incarnation, for the specter of the cross was there at Bethlehem. The marvel of God's becoming human is not just that God put on an infant's helplessness; nor is it that God assumed, for a time, our human limitations. No, the wonder of the Incarnation is that God became human even to taking on death. Only in that way could God become *completely* human, for death is an integral part of our life. To be born is to take the first step toward death.

Thus, what we are celebrating at the Incarnation is that the God-Who-Is chose to become a creature who would die. *That* is the wonder of Christmas!

And so, yes, death is here at Christmas. The manger scene takes place under the shadow of death; the historical Jesus, because he was born, would die. Christ's birth is the beginning of his life-death-resurrection journey, just as we begin our own death journey at birth. We can regard this life journey morbidly, or we can regard it joyfully and gratefully as the way in which we pass through life-in-time into life-in-eternity.

Does it seem inappropriate to speak of death at this season of joyous celebration of birth? "How sad for the family," someone is certain to say when a death occurs close to Christmas.

To those who are grieving now, we extend our sympathy; we assist them in bearing their grief. But we also recognize that, because of their loss, they are forced to look at the meaning of human existence—both in time and in eternity. And that is exactly what we are all called to do in this Incarnation Season: to view the whole of life. We look back at Christ's existence on earth and look forward to his coming at the end of time.

CONSIDER:

♦ What is my attitude toward death and Christmas?

♦ Do I know people who are in mourning this Incarnation Season? What can I do to let them know they have not been forgotten or abandoned? How might I help them still celebrate the Incarnation?

♦ Do I know people who have been grieving a loved one in recent years at this season? What can I do to let them know they and their loved ones have not been forgotten?

Celebrating Church

W hat is it about Christmas that draws people to church? Buildings that are sparsely filled the rest of the year are standing-room-only on Christmas (and Easter). People who are ordinarily embarrassed by the sacred come to church. Why?

Do people attend church on Christmas because they think it is expected of them? Are they responding to the inviting setting of decorations and flowers and special music? Is their attendance only the result of all the seasonal trappings?

Or could it be that the remotest possibility of the Incarnation being true—that God, Almighty God, became a human being—is so radical that it demands response? Could it be that people who hear very little of what the Churches say and do all year are so moved by the immensity of this idea—that God-made-human was born and died for us—that they bend head and knee in awe at the mere possibility of its being true?

What does this say about those of us who actually profess belief in such a thing? Every year, every week, every day, we affirm the truth of such a remarkable event. Because we have believed it for so long, has it lost its impact for us?

- ◆ What if the Incarnation never really happened? How would that affect my life?

- ◆ How does my celebration of the Incarnation reflect my beliefs?

- ◆ How does my life reflect my belief in the Incarnation?

- ◆ What can I do now to make this Incarnation Season a holy, happy, fulfilling one for me and for my family?

Celebrating Traditions

Traditions help us define who we are. ("We always go to Christmas Midnight Mass.") Traditions are our connection with the past and our legacy to the future. ("We always wait until after breakfast to look in our stockings.") They are a stabilizing factor in our lives, since they provide a sense of continuity in a time and culture dominated by change. ("Grandfather always says the table grace on Christmas.")

The importance of traditions often becomes painfully obvious when people marry, for the traditions of two different families are thus brought into potential conflict. ("Our family always strings popcorn for the tree.") Since traditions help define who we are, changes may be difficult, for some traditions may touch the core of our being. ("We always send photo Christmas greetings.") Thus the merging of the traditions of two families may entail difficult adjustments for all. ("On Christmas Eve Aunt Mable always sings 'O Holy Night' for the whole family.") The decision of whether to have a cut tree or an artificial tree may become a major family controversy. So also when to open presents, what kind of card to send, what to have for Christmas dinner, where to spend Christmas Eve, whether to exchange names for gifts, how to wrap and label gifts or....

And yet, sometimes traditions should be discontinued or changed. Since traditions help us define who we are, we should begin or continue those traditions that affirm us as individuals, strengthen family bonds, show love or add to the store of positive family memories. A permanent change in how we do things may come about by a tradition done only once!

CONSIDER:

♦ What are some of my family's traditions?

♦ Which one family tradition would be the hardest for me to abandon? Why?

♦ What new tradition would I like to establish in my family? How could I do this?

Celebrating Surprises

"**S**urprise!" The Archangel Gabriel might have begun his greeting to Mary with that word. Mary might have begun her announcement to Joseph in the same manner: "Surprise, Joseph—I'm pregnant!" "Surprised" probably could describe the reaction of the shepherds and the Magi when they came to worship the manger-born King. "Surprised" certainly is an understated description of the Jewish people's reaction to Jesus as the long-awaited Messiah.

There is an abundance of surprises in the Incarnation story that we can easily overlook because of our familiarity with the account. Nonetheless, the surprises are there, just as surprises have always been an integral part of salvation history.

Whenever humankind has tried to anticipate God's plan, we have encountered problems. God has had the habit of calling upon the lowly to lead and the inarticulate to preach. Providence seems to enjoy confusing us with blessings disguised as crosses; divine Wisdom's plots often involve making the first last and the last first. There is a sense of surprise in much of what God does.

Our part in this story of salvation history is to remain open to God's plan, for when life isn't progressing according to our design we may find ourselves encountering a divine surprise.

How fortunate we are! Not only is our God a God of love and mercy, but also a God with a sense of humor!

CONSIDER:

♦ How has the God of Surprises acted in my life?

♦ What has been my initial response to these surprises? My later response?

♦ Why is it often so difficult to accept these surprises?

Celebrating Symbols

I magine meeting someone who had never heard of Christ or Christianity. Imagine trying to explain to that individual the meanings of all the decorations and customs of the season! Let's see, there would be Santa Claus, Christmas trees, foods and drinks of all nationalities and ethnic origins, talking snowmen, mistletoe and holly and yule logs and wreaths, reindeer and sleighs, Christmas cookies and cards and candles and carols and concerts, bells and stars and candy canes, TV ads, decorative lights that blink or "travel," Rudolph and Scrooge and the Grinch.... And of course, there are mangers and kings and the Holy Family and angels and shepherds and animals of all sorts.

Some of these symbols have lost their original meaning; others have gained in significance. For symbols survive because of the multiplicity of their meanings. Some of the signs of the season are crass commercialism that, nonetheless, make our shopping easier. Others appear to be anti-Christian in their effects upon us. And still others are intimately and essentially connected to the meaning of the season. Yet all symbols falter in communicating the mysterious truth of the Incarnation.

It is left to us to use, ignore, destroy, highlight, fight, perpetuate, support, pass on, abuse and interpret the various symbols of the season.

CONSIDER:

♦ What symbols are especially meaningful to my family?

♦ Are there any Incarnation symbols that produce negative feelings in my family? In me?

♦ What would I like to change about this holiday time in my community? What would I like to change about this holiday time in my family? How could I go about doing that?

Celebrating Thanksgiving

How often now we are saying "thank you"! Thank you for the Christmas card, the gift, the cookies, the phone call, the story, the visit, the letter, the thoughtfulness.

And when we aren't busy expressing our own gratitude, we are reminding the kids of the accepted and expected etiquette of thankfulness: "Yes, you do have to write a thank-you note to your grandparents!"

It is right and proper to give thanks to others for their gifts, for their thoughtful acts of kindness, for their demonstrations of love. But it is also right and proper to give thanks to others for their most important gifts—the gifts of themselves: "Thank you for being you." And, of course, we have many reasons for thanking God. We are thankful for the taken-for-granted blessings: our senses, the beauty of nature, the goodness of others, our own talents and abilities. Here again, we can say "Thank you, God, for being you." And, finally, we can take a moment to say "Thank you, God, for creating me!"

CONSIDER:

♦ Who are the people in my life I would like to thank?

♦ Who are the people I take for granted? How can I let them know I am thankful that they are part of my life?

♦ What are some of the gifts from God I rarely think of or mention in thanksgiving?

Celebrating Visits

The biblical narratives of the Incarnation are filled with stories of visits: Gabriel visits Mary; Mary and Elizabeth have their touching visit; Joseph is called upon by an angelic messenger; Mary and Joseph visit Bethlehem; the shepherds visit the Babe; the angelic choirs visit Bethlehem; the Magi visit Herod and the family; the family visits the Temple in Jerusalem.

But it is the manger scene that remains the focus of our attention. Over the years, poets, songwriters and storytellers have added to the cast of visitors to Bethlehem, thereby demonstrating a persistent human fascination with being at that rough-made crib and seeing the newborn Christ Child. In our modern manger scene there may be a young boy with a drum, Santa Claus kneeling in prayer, a variety of birds and animals and trees and angels and snowmen and stars. All of creation longs to be there, for that manger scene sentimentalizes a human maturity untouched by the darkness, a maturity which, we know only too well, leads to a full adult life.

But the Gospel writers considered Christ's birth to be rather unimportant. They devoted little space to it, compared to the last days of his life. Approximately one-third of the Gospels details the events we celebrate at the Triduum (Holy Thursday, Good Friday and Easter).

If we were to ask a theologian to compare the importance of Christmas and Easter, we'd probably get a long dissertation about the significance of Easter compared to this feast of Christmas, for it is Easter that defines us as Christians. The celebration of Triduum, not the celebration of Christmas, is the high point of the entire liturgical year.

And yet, and yet—in spite of all these arguments, we would like to have been there at Bethlehem. It is easier to be sentimental about Christmas than about Easter. We do not have to endure a Good Friday in order to celebrate Christmas; Christmas has that delightful appeal to children and its emphasis upon family.

We nod our heads in agreement with the theologian's arguments about the importance of Easter—yes, yes, yes. But deep down we understand why Christ came first in that most approachable of human forms, a baby: to touch our hearts, to appeal to our emotions, to gain our love. That's why we would like to have been there at Bethlehem!

CONSIDER:

♦ What do I imagine the visitors at the manger said or thought or felt?

♦ What do I imagine the witnesses of the crucifixion said or thought or felt?

- What is the relative importance of these two feasts in my beliefs?

- What is the relative importance of these two feasts in my life?

Celebrating the Magi

The Magi are on their star-directed way to the newborn king; we shall celebrate their actual arrival on Epiphany.

We do not know much about these men; they were astrologers, men of nobility, but not kings. We don't even know for certain how many Magi there were, but tradition tells us there were three—three daring men of faith! They left their homes to follow a star which would lead them, they believed, to the king of the Jews. These were people willing to risk time, effort and money—and possibly the ridicule of others—for their beliefs.

They brought with them on their quest gifts—not items appropriate for a newborn baby but gifts "fit for a king": items treasured in their culture, things considered valuable in that society.

We know so little about the Magi that their presence in Scripture raises many questions for us: Did only these wise men see the star? Or were they the only ones who understood its meaning? Or perhaps, did only they have sufficient faith to make the journey? And when they finally arrived and saw the Child, how did they react? What happened to them later? Having achieved their goal, were they changed men?

CONSIDER:

♦ In my imagination, how do I fill in the details of the story of the Magi?

♦ If I had been one of the Magi, which of my tangible possessions would I have brought?

♦ If I were to offer to my God one of my intangible possessions, which would it be? Knowledge? Virtues? My good name or reputation? My talents?

♦ Thomas Aquinas said, "The things that we love tell us what we are." What is my reaction to that statement?

Celebrating Family

"**F**amilies" come in tremendous variety. Color is one of the categories we use to describe families: black and white and yellow and red—although the black is rarely black and the white certainly is not white; neither is the yellow daisy-hued nor is the red the color of fire engines.

Families come in many sizes and conformations. Families are moms and kids, or grandparents with their kids' kids. Families are parents and children, cousins clustered together; families are singles or house-parents and house-children or people gathered in community. Families are aliens huddled in a foreign land or prisoners confined together or victims of a common disaster. Families can be blood-related or tied together legally or united by common interests or allied by location or bonded by love.

When families worship, they send up prayers in a babel of language and a cacophony of sound; they bow and sign crosses and kneel and dance and stand and eat and sing and prostrate themselves and process and smoke and shout and keep silence.

Though families vary in appearance and composition and tradition and belief, there is but one Family, the Family of God. And when we look at similarities—at common hopes and dreams, at joys and pains that affect all, at widespread concerns and universal needs, at identical hungers and griefs and fears and at our same-Creator heritage, we see what unites families into one Family. And then we begin to see the Family resemblance: We are all made in the image of God.

CONSIDER:

♦ Who makes up my "family"?

♦ What differences in other people are easy for me to accept? What differences in other people are difficult for me to accept?

♦ How can individuals help to unite peoples? What can I do to help in the cause of universal understanding and world peace?

Celebrating Memory

O n this day, perhaps more than any other day of the year, we are aware of the passage of time. Another year is ending. This day, this month, this year shall never come again. In all of time and in all of timeless eternity, *now* shall never be repeated. As we prepare to end this year and begin another, we encounter the God of the Eternal Now.

On this day, perhaps more than any other day of the year, we are aware of two of God's greatest gifts to us. The first is the blessing of memory. Memory makes us human. Through memory we learn and communicate; through memory we recognize the significance of the people and events of the past; through memory we memorialize and do liturgy.

The other gift is the blessing of forgetfulness. On this last day of the year, we collect the unpleasant memories of the past year. We let these hurts, real or imagined, from friend and family become like ashes scattered in the winds of divine love. We let our disappointments become fertile ground for new hopes and dreams.

On this last day of the year we collect together all the pleasant, happy memories of the past. We let our achievements and accomplishments reflect God's glory, generosity and love. We enter the New Year surrounded by thoughts of good and memories of good and expectations of good.

CONSIDER:

♦ How can I go about forgetting hurtful recollections of the past?

♦ How can I learn to concentrate on the good and happy thoughts of the past?

♦ What difference does it make from now on whether I think about the pleasant memories or the unhappy memories?

♦ How important are my expectations of what is to come? Why?

Celebrating Mary

Today we celebrate Mary, the Model of the Church. Who is this Mary? What does she look like? How do we envision her?

Mary, the Model of the Church, is not the innocent, untried, naive young girl who, when confronted with the Archangel Gabriel's offer, takes a leap of faith. It is not the young mother holding her divine Son, just beginning her walk in mystery with her God. It is not the woman who stood at the foot of the cross, face etched with the pain of the crucifixion. It is not one of these Marys; rather it is the woman formed by all these experiences.

Mary, Model of the Church, is the older, accomplished woman who, together with the other disciples, waited faithfully in prayer after the Ascension. It is the courageous and daring Mary who was the first committed disciple of Christ. It is the perceptive Mary who knew intimately that the overshadowing of the Spirit is always followed by new life. It is the hospitable, concerned Mary, the Jewish grandmother of all the Church. It is the understanding Mary who was teacher, helper, supporter of those first Christians and who continues to be teacher, helper, supporter of all who follow. It is this wise, loving,

tried-and-not-found-wanting Mary who is the Model of
the Church—our model.

CONSIDER:

♦ What is my most common image of Mary?

♦ How do I feel about envisioning her as an old
woman?

♦ How do I envision her relationship with the new
Christians? What might she have told them?

♦ What can Mary teach me?

Epiphany

Celebrating God-Made-Manifest

C hristians recognized early the importance of Epiphany, of God-Made-Manifest, for the celebration of Epiphany predates that of Christmas. This ancient feast has been known throughout the ages by various names: the Feast of Kings, Twelfth Night, The Last Day of Christmas. January 6, the traditional date for the celebration of Epiphany, follows the twelve days of Christmas. (Begin counting on the day after Christmas.)

During Advent we anticipated the comings of Christ; during the Christmas Season we celebrated his historical coming with both activities and times of quiet. As Epiphany comes, we have no reason for gloom or for post-holiday depression, for it is only now that we can celebrate the fullness of the entire season. Only now has the Incarnation Season come full cycle. Epiphany is the fullness of the Incarnation.

We are celebrating not simply the arrival of those men of mystery, the Magi, but the manifestation of God to everyone! All history has been preparation for this feast when we recognize, accept and proclaim the wonderment of God-Made-Flesh. Christ has come! Maranatha! Christ is here, within us, around us. We proclaim the gospel message of justice and love to all.

Today we celebrate the God of glory—alleluia! We celebrate Emmanuel—God with us!

♦ What difference do I see between Christmas and Epiphany?

♦ How can I celebrate Epiphany?

♦ When am I most aware of the presence of God in the world?

♦ When am I most aware of the presence of God in my life?

A Time of Preaching

One day St. Francis of Assisi invited a friend to preach with him. The two brothers left the monastery and began to stroll the streets of Assisi. Francis never passed a person without extending a cheerful greeting. The kids got a hug and an eye-level smile. The mothers with babes in arms received compliments on their beautiful offspring. He wished merchants well, welcomed newcomers to Assisi and listened to the elderly with respect.

Eventually Francis and the young man arrived back at the monastery. The puzzled brother asked why they had not preached.

"We preached as we walked" was the answer of gentle Francis.

Epiphany is the time when we proclaim to the

world what we are celebrating. Some of us are called to proclaim in sermon or written form the story of God's love; some of us are called to proclaim it in words to students or to our children; but all of us are called to proclaim the story in our lives.

CONSIDER:

♦ How might Francis walk through *my* day?

♦ What beliefs about the Incarnation might be construed from "listening" to the preaching of my actions?

♦ How effective is this kind of preaching?

A Time of Reality

What is reality?
Often, at times of high emotion, or celebration, we tend to say, "But this isn't reality," as though reality can only mean boredom or routine.

Mary understood reality, whether we are referring to the reality of high emotion or the reality of routine or the reality of awareness. That woman whom we so often represent in unbending plastic or unyielding marble or on untouchable canvas knew reality.

Every pregnant woman knows reality. She knows

the reality of her own body and that of the child within her. What may begin as intellectual knowledge of pregnancy gradually becomes transformed into acute awareness. Eventually the woman knows, with every breath she breathes, in every movement of her body, during every moment of her existence, the reality of the other within her.

This awareness culminates in the all-consuming reality of childbirth, when the reality of the here and now becomes so intense as to obliterate everything in the universe except that woman, her baby and the miracle of giving birth. In that mystical moment of birthing, of pain and joy and exhilaration, that woman knows intimately the reality of life and creation. The ultimate reality is God.

Did Mary, having given birth to the God-Child, wonder what more life could possibly contain for her? Did she, following that intense intimacy with reality, wonder if anything here on earth could ever be felt or experienced again? Perhaps that is why God sent glorious choirs of angels—not to the shepherds so much as to Mary, who needed the consolation of heavenly singing to help her remain on earth.

Mary did indeed remain. And after all the heavenly and earthly visitors, all the miraculous happenings, Mary's life took on the reality of obscurity and routine. Mary and Joseph and the Holy Child spent their days doing daily things.

CONSIDER:

- What is real? The miracle of the Incarnation? The miracle of birth—any birth?

- When am I most aware of the reality of life, of my existence? Why then?

- How do I balance my expectations with reality?

- When do I experience the reality of God? How?

- When does Christ seem most real to me: as an infant, as a young boy, as a teacher and healer, on the cross, as the risen Christ?

A Time of Storytelling

At all times, always, we celebrate stories! Now, of course, we are celebrating the wonderful, joyful Incarnation. This is but a single chapter of the story of salvation history, which continues to be written, as it will until Judgment Day.

It is through the age-old custom of storytelling that our forefathers and foremothers once again come alive. It is through storytelling that we provide nourishment to the young to develop the roots they need through life. It is through storytelling that we help them discover who they are, for the past has helped form them.

We also celebrate the stories of today, by telling, in our own particular words and in our own particular time and for our own particular generation, how God has worked—and continues to work—now. God is here: in and among us. And when we tell our story, we are adding this chapter to the salvation history story. We tell the story to our family as we recount our day around the dinner table. We tell the story to our coworkers at coffee breaks and in the carpool. We tell the story to our friends in our letters and phone calls. Our story is unveiled in the current chapter of the complete story of salvation history.

And, of course, we listen. We listen to the stories of others, to see how God is working in their lives. Together, in our telling and in our listening, we celebrate *us*! We celebrate our stories!

CONSIDER:

♦ What is my favorite Incarnation story? Why?

♦ What is my favorite Incarnation memory? Why?

♦ What, so far, is most memorable about this Incarnation season? Why?

♦ What is my story? How do I view my story as part of salvation history?

A Time of Time

New Testament Greek uses two different words for time. One is *chronos*, from which we get the words *chronometer* and *chronology*. In chronos time every second is counted: It is the time we spend standing on aching legs at the check-out counter; it is empty time, time we "pass" or try to "fill." Chronos time is impersonal.

But *kairos* time is different. If chronos time is empty, then kairos time is full. If chronos time is the time which we humans count, then kairos is God's time; the time when God is present—and we are aware of that presence; it is "Epiphany." The New Testament Christians experienced a sense of kairos time, the proper time in which God has set forth a new dimension of reality: "This is the time of fulfillment!" (Mark 1:15). Kairos time is the occasion of insight, of revelation, of inspiration, of love. We do not count kairos time, and when we speak of kairos time it is in poetic or paradoxical terms: "Time stood still" or "We were transported out of time." Kairos time is remembered and understood not by our intellect but by our intuition. We speak of it only afterward, for only then do we realize we have been in another time. It is in kairos time that we find the meaning of life and love, of our relationships with each other and with God.

The Judeo-Christian religion has long recognized that time is a creation of and a gift from God. The Liturgy of the Hours proclaims the holiness of each day in Morning Prayer and Evening Prayer. The liturgical year is the Church's way of recognizing the holiness of the seasons and the year. By means of feasts and liturgies, the Church tries to alert us to kairos time. While kairos time can intrude upon our lives, usually it occurs only if we make room for it. We must be open to those moments of insight, of new learning, of love offered, of opportunities available, of happiness between two people, of God.

CONSIDER:

♦ When do I experience chronos time?

♦ When do I experience kairos time?

♦ How can I make more room in my life for kairos time?

A Time of Visions

The entire Incarnation Season is a time of visions. It began with visions of sugar plums and decorated trees capping mountains of presents. We enjoyed visions of Santa who, with only minor assistance from a few workaholic elves and various reindeer, manages to circle the globe in one night. We have enjoyed visions of friends and family gathered together for holiday feasts of grand scale.

Many of our visions came into being, for only that which begins as a vision, as a dream or a hope, will ever come to be. What we don't dream will never be. As we read the great peace-proclaiming readings of Isaiah, as we proclaim the coming of the Cosmic Christ, our focus turns to peace. The Incarnation is the celebration of peace.

Of course, we do not have world peace yet. But if we do not envision it, dream of it, we can be sure it will never happen.

It is not enough that we pray for world peace. We must work for world peace. And for our prayers—and our efforts—to be effective, we must believe wholeheartedly in the possibility of our intentions. If we don't envision it, however, if we don't affirm it, it will never occur. So let us help bring about world peace by affirming its presence in the world, now, today.

CONSIDER:

♦ How firmly do I believe in my prayer intentions?

♦ How does my affirming world peace help bring it into existence?

♦ What is my vision of world peace?

♦ What can I do today to help bring about world peace?

A Time of Secrets Revealed

We have completed a time of secrets, both in Scripture and in our own recent experience. The handmade gifts have been completed; the carefully concealed and wrapped presents have been brought forth and opened. The "secret pals" have been revealed and the surprise visits and trips have occurred.

We have celebrated the secrets surrounding Mary's and Elizabeth's pregnancies. All the secret nativity visits of angels are completed. The Magi have taken their secret way home and we have read of the Holy Family's secret, hurried trip to Egypt.

All these things have been made known. And now the greatest secret is revealed by Paul in his Letter to the Ephesians, read on the feast of the Epiphany: "[T]he Gentiles are coheirs, members of the same body, and copartners in the promise in Christ Jesus through the gospel" (Ephesians 3:6).

That is God's surprise: Salvation is available to all of us! And it is to remain secret no longer. It is given to us to spread this—the Good News—to others; we are to do this both by deed and by word. This is the Good News for which we began our preparations that First Sunday of Advent.

CONSIDER:

♦ How did I learn of God's "secret plan"?

♦ If I were God, what would be my plan for salvation?

♦ What are the differences in my plan and what I perceive as God's plan?

♦ How can I help make known this "secret"?

Ordinary Time: A Time of Growth and Proclamation

"The beginning of the gospel of Jesus Christ [the Son of God]" (Mark 1:1). And where does Mark, the first of the evangelists to set down a Gospel in writing, begin his narrative? At the baptism of Christ!

Only later, in response to requests for background information, did Matthew and Luke provide for us the Infancy Narratives. Those stories of events surrounding Christ's birth, however, are but a prelude to what begins with his baptism, when once again the Holy Spirit descends, as at the Annunciation. And once again, there is new life, the new life of Christ's public ministry. In time the Holy Spirit will descend at Pentecost, and then the Church will be born. The Spirit, the "Go-between-God," brings life!

This celebration of Christ's baptism launches us with renewed vigor into our own vocation of carrying the gospel message of Christ. We recall our own baptism as the beginning of our ministry of proclamation. What we have celebrated during this entire Incarnation season we must now proclaim through word and deed.

The Church refers to our time of proclamation as

"Ordinary Time." But Ordinary Time is not the lull between high-ritual events; Ordinary Time is not empty time, chronos time, with which the Church fills up the liturgical year. The Gospel readings during this "ordinary" time are filled with parables and miracles. Scripture continues the story of salvation history, the story of God's love for us. Indeed, it is a most extraordinary time!

It is during this Ordinary Time that the Church and Christ remind us of the sacramentality of everyday life—the really real! The Scriptures tell us of the importance of what we do on the "ordinary" day by recounting stories of parents and housewives and farmers and managers and children. They tell us stories about preparing meals and sowing seed and having guests, of losing and finding and celebrating and traveling and repenting and loving. The Church and Christ remind us of the sacredness of the daily because that is where growth occurs. We grow through routine ways and during ordinary times. We grow through the presence of the Holy Spirit. We grow, and by our growth we carry out our ministry to spread the Good News. The reign of God is here, now!

CONSIDER:

♦ How have I grown during this past Incarnation Season? This past year?

♦ How do I recognize the sacredness of the ordinary in my life? When am I most aware of the sacramentality of the everyday?

♦ How can I proclaim the gospel in my life?

♦ What can I do to help bring about the reign of God?

Incarnation Season Projects and Gifts

Projects for Families and Individuals

♦ Plan Incarnation Season TV-viewing thoughtfully.

♦ Write an Incarnation story or poem.

♦ Make an Advent-Christmas record book to keep. Include journal entries, pictures from magazines and newspapers, quotes from cards or carols, names of visitors, moments of inspiration, memorable events, Scripture texts. (This is a family project to which all ages can contribute.)

♦ Periodically ask yourself the question: "What can I personally do to make this Incarnation Season more enjoyable and more holy for my family?"

♦ Make a Jesse Tree: "[A] shoot shall sprout from the stump of Jesse,/ and from his roots a bud shall blossom" (Isaiah 11:1). Hang on a large tree branch or place on a banner scriptural symbols from Jesus' family tree.

♦ Research Christmas customs and Incarnation Season projects of different ethnic groups, and especially those of your own heritage.

♦ Reclaim a tradition from your ethnic heritage.

♦ Choose a new tradition to do as an individual during this Incarnation Season.

♦ Choose a new family tradition for this year.

♦ Drop from your activities this year one holiday tradition that has lost its meaning for you.

♦ On an especially hectic day, take time to reflect on the meaning of the Incarnation Season.

♦ Design or make your own Christmas cards.

♦ While writing letters, addressing packages, signing cards and stamping envelopes, pray for each person or family.

♦ Sing or recite all the verses of an appropriate Advent, Christmas or Epiphany hymn or song as part of family prayer-time or as a table grace. (Inexpensive hymn/song sheets or collections are usually available at music stores, bookstores, religious articles shops or the Christmas section of department stores.)

♦ Have a family get-together with a purpose: to make taffy or spaghetti sauce or cookies or Advent wreaths or....

- Have a multigenerational family get-together, with storytelling and photo-sharing as the main entertainment.

- Tape-record or video-record the memories of the oldest members of the family.

- Offer rides to church to friends and neighbors during the Incarnation season.

- Include prayer, Scripture-reading or meditation on the "to-do" list.

- Read the assigned Scriptures for each day.

- Pray the rosary, meditating on the joyful mysteries.

- Give up a favorite grudge.

- Get involved in a project to help the homeless or needy during this season.

- Adopt, anonymously, a needy family, by giving gifts, sending notes of encouragement and praying.

♦ Decorate for *Advent!* Include dark blue-violet, the color of Advent, and evergreens, a symbol of eternal life.

♦ Use an Advent calendar. (Many lovely Advent calendars are available at card counters, while homemade ones are always special.)

♦ Have a home Advent wreath and use it at mealtime or prayer time (see page 123).

♦ Contribute toys to Santa Anonymous, Toys for Tots or other organizations devoted to providing toys for needy children on Christmas.

♦ Help children become aware of the poor and needy by helping them contribute to Santa Anonymous, Toys for Tots or other such organizations.

♦ Attend a communal celebration of the Sacrament of Reconciliation.

♦ Fast or abstain during Advent in joyful anticipation of Christ's coming and as a way of making room for God in your life.

♦ When you encounter impolite or rude people, pause and say a prayer for them, blessing them in their time of impatience.

- Greet everyone you meet with the thought "The gracious Christ in me greets the Christ in you."

- Observe the Northern European custom of being a "Kriss Kringle"—a secret giver of gifts. Throughout Advent, pray especially for the chosen person and provide surprises and humorous gifts for that individual. On Christmas give the real gift and reveal your identity. (This custom is suitable for individuals, families or groups.)

FOR THE DAYS OF CHRISTMAS:

- Have a Christ Candle for the Christmas/Epiphany Seasons.

- Choose one or more ways to celebrate in a special way the Christmas Season—the time from Christmas to Epiphany.

- Send Christmas cards during the *Christmas* Season rather than the Advent Season.

- Have a home Thanksgiving Service. (This is especially appropriate during this season, when we are often giving thanks for *things* and forgetting to be thankful for *people* and the gifts they are to us. See page 130.)

- Write thank-you notes to the people who have helped make the past year memorable.

- Have a "thank you" party and write thank-you notes.

- Make a list of "taken-for-granted" gifts such as life, sight, freedom, mobility, opportunity.

- Make a list of blessings.

- Bless your children, your parents, your spouse, other relatives, friends, coworkers, the ill and dying....

- Bless the Christmas tree during Advent (see page 129).

- Make a list of all the various symbols of the season encountered each day.

- Discuss with the family the meanings of the various symbols of the season.

- During family time together, read aloud the Christmas cards received.

- On New Year's Eve or Day, write down, on separate pieces of paper, all the incidents of unpleasantness, worry or hurt from the past year. Then burn them, one by one. As they are consumed, bless the people involved while placing the memories of the hurts in the hands of God.

♦ Have an Epiphany party.

♦ Have an Epiphany house dedication and blessing (see page 133).

♦ Make arrangements now to visit the lonely during the January-February "blahs." (Often nursing homes, hospitals, shelters for the homeless and senior centers have many visitors and entertainment groups who come *before* Christmas.)

♦ Plant a narcissus, crocus or amaryllis bulb to brighten someone's home/room/life after the holidays.

♦ Introduce a family discussion on the sacredness of everyday life.

♦ As the Magi took another way home following their visit to the Holy Family, choose different routes to your usual destinations.

♦ Discuss with friends or family or write in your journal about how this Incarnation Season has changed you.

Projects for Groups and Organizations

♦ Plan an activity to help others prepare for Christmas, such as taking an elderly or differently abled person shopping, decorating a nursing home.

♦ Adopt, anonymously, a needy family. Give gifts, send notes of encouragement and pray.

♦ Get involved in a project to help the homeless or needy during this season.

♦ Instead of having a gift-exchange, buy gifts for the needy.

♦ Choose a project which helps to bring about the reign of God, such as a social justice concern.

♦ Make a booklet of Incarnation Season memories, poems, meditations and artwork contributed by members. Copies of this booklet can be gifts to the members, to the parish or to the organization.

♦ Plan a post-holiday visit to a nursing home, hospital or senior center to sing, entertain or just talk with the residents.

Gift Suggestions

For somehow, not only at Christmas, but all the
  long year through,
The joy that you give to others is the joy that
  comes back to you. —John Greenleaf Whittier

FOR EVERYONE AND ANYONE:

♦ Instead of buying a gift, show love! Through a
  special act or deed or word, bring Christ's love to
  someone.

♦ Give others increased joy by receiving their gifts
  with enthusiastic appreciation and gratitude.

♦ Consider giving a present at a time other than
  Christmas. Holiday items given on Thanksgiving or
  on the Feast of St. Nicholas (December 6) will add
  to the recipient's enjoyment of the season. The
  summer solstice, St. Patrick's Day, Easter, the
  beginning of school or of the planting season,
  Mother's Day and Father's Day all offer
  opportunities for especially appreciated gifts.

♦ Give gifts of thoughts. A thought-gift can be given
  verbally or in written form. It can be an idea, an
  expression of appreciation or love, a reassurance of
  faith in the individual, an uplifting or consoling
  thought, a reminder of forgotten dreams, an
  affirming expression of hope. As Christ brings hope
  to humanity, so we can give hope to one another.

- Give the gift of being needed by making your needs and vulnerability known to another.

- Give a prayer gift, praying either *with* or *for* another.

- Give gifts of self: a hair-set or a massage, grass-cutting or snow-shoveling, a home-cooked meal.

- Give to the needy instead of having a gift exchange.

FOR THE HARD TO PLEASE OR THE
PERSON WHO 'HAS EVERYTHING':

- Make a *thoughtfully chosen* contribution in that person's name to:

  the local symphony orchestra, park, zoo, hospital or library;

  the missions;

  the Humane Society or the Audubon Society;

  a wildlife preservation group or an ecology organization;

  the U.S. Olympic team or the Special Olympics;

  American Heart Association, American Cancer Society;

  UNICEF;

  an organization dedicated to relieving world hunger;

  an organization dedicated to helping people with disabilities;

  a church building or organ fund;

the recipient's high school or college;

any charity of special interest to the individual.

FOR THE HOMEBOUND OR THE FINANCIALLY DISTRESSED:

♦ Give an early Christmas gift consisting of items that
person can give to others: holiday candies, small
boxes of Christmas goodies, stationery, decorated
mugs, bookmarks, gourmet coffees or teas,
calendars, food items, children's books and toys.
Consider including wrapping paper and ribbon.

FOR YOURSELF:

♦ Take time to remind yourself that you are loved.

♦ Take time to remind yourself that you are worthy
and worthwhile.

♦ Take time to remind yourself of the reasons we
celebrate the Incarnation Season.

FOR SPECIAL PEOPLE:

♦ One gift that only you can give is your story.
Consider sharing memories with close family and
friends. This is especially appropriate for the
elderly and for those who have helped shape your
life. Share a Christmas memory, the story of

someone's influence in your life, and so on. This can be done with several others and made into a joint gift. Add photos and mementos.

♦ Give a thank-you gift to a parent or relative or especially close friend: Write the story of that person's influence on your life.

♦ Give the gift of a happy memory. Recall for someone, by word or by letter, a pleasant or inspiring memory.

Prayers for the Incarnation Season

Biblical Prayers

THE CANTICLE OF MARY (THE MAGNIFICAT)

My soul proclaims the greatness of the Lord;
  my spirit rejoices in God my savior.
For he has looked upon his handmaid's lowliness;
  behold, from now on will all ages call me blessed.
The Mighty One has done great things for me,
  and holy is his name.
His mercy is from age to age
  to those who fear him.
He has shown might with his arm,
  dispersed the arrogant of mind and heart.
He has thrown down the rulers from their thrones
  but lifted up the lowly.
The hungry he has filled with good things;
  the rich he has sent away empty.
He has helped Israel his servant,
  remembering his mercy,
according to his promise to our fathers,
  to Abraham and to his descendants forever.
(Luke 1:46b-55)

Blessed be the Lord, the God of Israel,
    for he has visited and brought redemption to his
        people.
He has raised up a horn for our salvation
    within the house of David his servant,
even as he promised through the mouth
    of his holy prophets from of old:
    salvation from our enemies and from the hand of
        all who hate us,
to show mercy to our fathers
    and to be mindful of his holy covenant
and of the oath he swore to Abraham our father,
    and to grant us that, rescued from the hand of
        enemies,
without fear we might worship him in holiness and
        righteousness
    before him all our days.
And you, child, will be called prophet of the Most
        High,
    for you will go before the Lord to prepare his ways,
to give his people knowledge of salvation
    through the forgiveness of their sins,
because of the tender mercy of our God
    by which the daybreak from on high will visit us
to shine on those who sit in darkness and death's
        shadow,
    to guide our feet into the path of peace.
(Luke 1:68-79)

The people who walked in darkness
    have seen a great light;
Upon those who dwelt in the land of gloom
    a light has shown.
You have brought them abundant joy
    and great rejoicing,
As they rejoice before you as at the harvest,
    as men make merry when dividing spoils.
For the yoke that burdened them,
    the pole on their shoulder,
And the rod of their taskmaster
    you have smashed, as on the day of Midian.
For every boot that trampled in battle,
    every cloak rolled in blood,
    will be burned as fuel for flames.
For a child is born to us, a son is given us;
    upon his shoulder dominion rests.
They name him Wonder-Counselor, God-Hero,
    Father-Forever, Prince of Peace.
His dominion is vast
    and forever peaceful,
From David's throne, and over his kingdom,
    which he confirms and sustains
By judgment and justice,
    both now and forever.
The zeal of the LORD of Hosts will do this!
(Isaiah 9:1-6)

CANTICLE OF THE ANGELS

Glory to God in the highest
and on earth peace to those on whom
his favor rests. (Luke 2:14)

CANTICLE OF SIMEON

Now, Master, you may let your servant go
in peace, according to your word,
for my eyes have seen your salvation,
which you prepared in sight of all the peoples,
a light for revelation to the Gentiles,
and glory for your people Israel. (Luke 2:29-32)

Traditional Prayers

THE HAIL MARY

Hail Mary, full of grace,
the Lord is with you.
Blessed are you among women
and blessed is the fruit of your womb, Jesus.
Holy Mary, mother of God,
pray for us sinners,
now and at the hour of our death. Amen.

THE ANGELUS

(Traditionally, this prayer is recited three times a day: six a.m., noon and six p.m. When the Angelus is prayed while standing, it is also tradition to genuflect at the words: "And the word became flesh and dwelt among us.")

Verse: The angel spoke God's message to Mary,

Response: and she conceived of the Holy Spirit.

Hail, Mary....

V: "I am the lowly servant of the Lord:"

R: "let it be done to me according to your word."

Hail, Mary....

V: And the word became flesh,

R: and lived among us.

Hail, Mary....

V: Pray for us, holy Mother of God,

R: that we may become worthy of the promises of Christ.

Let us pray:

Lord, fill our hearts with your grace:
once, through the message of an angel
you revealed to us the Incarnation of your Son;
now, through his suffering and death,
lead us to the glory of his Resurrection.
We ask this through Christ our Lord.

R. Amen.

THE JOYFUL MYSTERIES OF THE ROSARY

1) The Annunciation

2) The Visitation

3) The Nativity

4) The Presentation

5) The Finding in the Temple

Seasonal Prayers

THE ADVENT WREATH

The Advent wreath is a beautiful and ancient family tradition that is still meaningful to us today as we count down to Christmas.

The wreath may be purchased or homemade. Four candles are placed in a circle, which may then be decorated with greenery, usually evergreen boughs. Both the circle and the evergreens symbolize eternity or eternal life.

One candle is lit on the First Sunday of Advent and relit each day throughout the first week. On the Second Sunday of Advent, the adjoining candle is lit, and throughout the second week these two candles are used. On each of the next two Sundays another candle is lit, so that during the Fourth Week of Advent all four candles are burning. A prayer or meditation is often part of the lighting ceremony.

Sometimes a fifth candle is included in the Advent wreath. This candle, which is placed in the center of the wreath, represents Christ and is used on Christmas.

The liturgical color of Advent is purple, except for the Third Sunday, when the color is rose, a reminder to us to be joyful. This same color scheme is often used for Advent wreath candles. With today's emphasis on waiting and anticipation, dark blue-violet, the predawn color, is appropriate for the wreath candles. White is always acceptable, too.

ADVENT WREATH PRAYERS

The Advent wreath is not a liturgical symbol—that is, it is not an official part of the Church's rituals or liturgies. The fact that it has endured and even grown in popularity indicates its value to both families and individuals. Since there are no "official" prayers, each family may adapt it for its own use.

A family with young children may decide to use the Hail Mary for the lighting prayer, thus teaching the prayer to the children and using it to begin discussions about the Incarnation. The first words are the Angel Gabriel's address to Mary at the Annunciation. They are followed by Elizabeth's greeting to Mary at the Visitation. These two events are the first two joyful mysteries of the rosary. The Hail Mary ends with our own words of petition to Mary. In this way, young children learn the Hail Mary, discuss the coming of Jesus, the rosary and the Joyful Mysteries of the rosary (see page 123).

An individual or a family with older children may choose to use a prayer or Scripture reading that concerns the Incarnation, such as the Magnificat (see page 118), the "O Antiphons" (page 132) or the Angelus (page 122).

An individual or a family may choose to sing or read an Advent hymn.

Or use the following prayers:

First Week

Hush. Be still.
Advent is a quiet season,
   a time for prayer,
   a time for meditation.
Advent is a time for marveling
   at inner mysteries,
   at hidden secrets,
   at life itself.
Advent is a time for watching
   in awed silence.
Advent is a time for waiting
   in Mary-like faithfulness.

O Gentle God of stillness,
   let this candle,
   which we now light,
   be a mute summons to prayer.
Help our wondering,
   our yearning,
   our seeking.

You, Divine Mystery,
  became human to be with us.
In mystery no less divine,
  we are called to be with you!
In patient faith, we pray:

Come, O Word divine!

RESPONSE: Come, O Word divine!

Second Week

Advent is a family season.
It is a time of closeness,
  of interdependence,
  of bountiful love extended.
Especially now do we affirm family:
  those of home and heart,
  those of our parish and community,
  those in struggle and in pain,
  and everyone in God's incredibly diverse
    family.
With letters and cards and presents,
  with the generosity of our hearts,
  with the music of our lives,
  with spontaneous love,
  we celebrate family!

Creator of the Universe,
  let these candles,
  which we now light,
  remind us that we are your children.
In love you created the human family

and all that was,
   is,
   and will be.
Yet you, who are our Creator,
   are also our brother!
And so in awestruck wonder we pray:

Come, O Love divine!

RESPONSE: Come, O Love divine!

Third Week

Joyful, joyful!
How overflowing with joy is Advent!
It is a time of activity—
   of cradle-making and shopping,
   of traveling,
   of preparing swaddling clothes
   and make-ahead foods,
   of celebrating the gift of life!
Advent is a time of expectation—
   of preparing for Christ's birth,
   of proclaiming our faith
   in Christ's second coming.
In Christ is our joy!

O God of darkness and light,
   let this candle,
   which we now light,
   remind us of the wonder of Christ.
In you is gladness!
In you we find our fulfillment
   and the abundance of joy.

In excited anticipation of new life
  we exclaim:

Come, O Light divine!

RESPONSE: Come, O Light divine!

Fourth Week

Advent is a season of openness and hope.
It is a time of trusting—
  trusting in divine goodness,
  and in the goodness of each other.
As Advent draws to a close
  we recognize that Christmas—
  and Christ's presence—
  may not be what we expect.
God, who delights in surprises,
  calls us to openness.
Only if we are open
  can we recognize
  a Messiah in a newborn baby,
  a Savior in a condemned criminal,
  the Christ present in each of *us*!

O God of hopeful surprises
  and surprising hope,
  let these candles,
  which we now light,
  open our hearts to you.
You have surrounded us with your love!
Help us respond to that love.
And may we remember, O God,
  during this busy season,

that as we greet each other,
we are greeting you,
who are truly present in us all.

Come, O God-Made-Manifest!

RESPONSE: Come, O God-Made-Manifest!

BLESSING OF THE CHRISTMAS TREE

God of the Universe,
　　Creator of glimmering stars and shining planets,
　　Originator of rainbows,
　　Lover of children:
　　bless this, our Christmas tree.

It is in celebration of Christ's coming
　　that we have decorated this tree
　　with angels and toys and glistening balls.
May its beauty refresh our souls
　　and bring joy and love to our home.

As our tree points heavenward,
　　may its presence remind us, O God,
　　of your presence in our home
　　and in our lives.

(The blessing may be concluded by singing
"O Christmas Tree.")

Leader: Creator God, Source of all that is,
    Giver of all good gifts,
    we thank you for your generosity to us.
You have given us life,
    and all that we need to live life abundantly;
You have given us your son
    and the richness of the gospel message.
And you have given us each other,
    with our talents and abilities.
We thank you now, God,
    for ourselves and for each other.
In recognizing our gifts,
    we recognize you as the Giver.
In expressing our gratitude to each other,
    we honor you.

We recognize the gift of N.,
    and blessings that N. brings to us,
    especially *(name talents, abilities, personality traits)*.
Thank you, God, for N.

All: Thank you, God, for N.

(Repeat for each person.)

Leader: We thank you, God,
    for each person in our home,
    our community, our world.
In our thanksgiving,
    we begin to see each other
    as you, our Creator, see us.
We begin to recognize that we are all
    bearers of your love to one another. Amen.

CHRISTMAS GIFTS

There is nothing I can give you
Which you have not;
But there is much that,
While I cannot give, you can take.

No heaven can come to us
Unless our hearts find rest in it today.
Take heaven.

No peace lies in the future
Which is not hidden in this present instant.
Take peace.

The gloom of the world is but a shadow;
Behind it, yet within reach, is joy.
Take joy.

And so, at this Christmastime,
I greet you with the prayer that for you,
Now and forever,
The daybreak and the shadows flee away.

—Fra Giovanni

O Wisdom, O holy Word of God, you govern all creation with your strong yet tender care. Come and show your people the way to salvation.

O Sacred Lord of ancient Israel, who showed yourself to Moses in the burning bush, who gave him the holy law on Sinai mountain: come, stretch out your mighty hand to set us free.

O Flower of Jesse's stem, you have been raised up as a sign for all peoples; kings stand silent in your presence; the nations bow down in worship before you. Come, let nothing keep you from coming to our aid.

O Key of David, O royal Power of Israel controlling at your will the gate of heaven: come, break down the prison walls of death for those who dwell in darkness and the shadow of death; and lead your captive people into freedom.

O Radiant Dawn, splendor of eternal light, sun of justice: come, shine on those who dwell in darkness and the shadow of death.

O King of all the nations, the only joy of every human heart; O Keystone of the mighty arch of [humanity], come and save the creature you fashioned from the dust.

O Emmanuel, king and lawgiver, desire of the nations, Savior of all people, come and set us free, Lord our God.

—Liturgy of the Hours

BLESSING OF A HOME

Loving God, you whose home is everywhere,
bless this, our (my) home.

Bless the doorways and rooms,
the windows and floors and lights.

Let all who dwell here
be sheltered from every harm and lack.

Let all who eat and work and play and rest here
enjoy wholeness of mind and body.

Let all who speak and read and pray here
be affirmed as sacred to you.

Let all who come here
find forgiveness, love, and peace.

We pray this blessing
in the name of the Creator,
the Savior and the Sustainer.
Amen.